ARTISAN
PIZZA

TO MAKE PERFECTLY AT HOME

GIUSEPPE MASCOLI
& BRIDGET HUGO

Kyle Books

CONTENTS

Intro   6

ESSENTIALS   8
Equipment   10
Dough   12
Tomato   20
Cheese   22
Oils & Fats   23

PIZZAS   24

Resources   124
Index   126
Acknowledgments   128

INTRODUCTION

When you find yourself eating in a Neopolitan pizzeria watching the skilled artisans working with flour, water, and a few local ingredients, you are the latest in a very long line of customers. Pizza is the ultimate delicious, fast, affordable meal—one that was enjoyed by our ancestors in Ancient Greece and Persia. Archeological evidence found in Pompeii also shows that, in the 1st century AD, round flatbreads, cooked with rosemary, oil, garlic, cheese, and anchovies, were being made in a wood-fired oven by a local baker, Podiscus Pricus, who sold them on a street near the Forum. A smaller oven, four feet in diameter, dating from the 2nd century AD, has also been discovered in the Greco-Roman market area of Naples. Less than a quarter of the size of the Pompeian one, it is not ideal for bread but is perfect for pizza. Located in the retail area of the town, in what today would be called the main street, the "pizzas" made here, like those in Pompeii, were sold as street food.

Pizza remained solely street food until the late 18th century. Port'Alba, which began selling pizzas in Naples in 1787, added an interior seating area in 1830, becoming the first "pizzeria." Alexander Dumas ate there in 1835, noting that, "in Naples, pizza is flavored with oil, lard, tallow, cheese, tomato, or anchovies." With the exception of tomato, these are the same ingredients that were being used 2,000 years earlier. Today, Port'Alba still operates on the same premises and continues to follow the same successful business plan.

Inevitably, in the 20th century, pizza fell victim to the fast food trend. What is too often offered on Main Street today is far more corporate and industrial than local. Long fermentation has been abandoned for a fast-developing product. Dough is centrally produced, mechanically divided, and frozen. The sourcing of the ingredients is globalized. Processed cheeses have taken the place of the short-lasting but long-tasting *fior di latte* or mozzarella. Skilled artisans have been replaced by semiskilled workers transferring defrosted dough into a pan. Occasionally, "entertainers" are hired to spin the dough in the air (something you will never see in Naples) to deceive the customers about the true nature of their operation.

Supermarkets also stack their shelves with precooked pizzas topped with globally sourced ingredients of uncertain provenance. The collapse of trading barriers between countries has furthered the rush for cheaper products. In this situation the customer is ever more removed from the producer, the retailer, and the stove.

Franco Manca was built on the belief that, although there are many ways of eating, to be truly enjoyed, food needs to be made with integrity and with authentic ingredients. When we opened the first Franco Manca restaurant in London in 2008, we were fighting against the tide. Between 1985 and 1989, it had been a pizzeria owned by Franco Pensa and was called simply Franco. It was a legendary place, loved by the locals and mentioned in a number of books, including Geoff Dyer's *The Color of Memory*, and we were determined to honor its legacy. So we decided to call it Franco *Manca*. A common Italian surname, Manca also means "missing," so Franco Manca means "missing Franco" or "Franco is missing."

We had a wood oven built by one of the great Neapolitan artisans, Mastro Ciccio, and we trained local producers to make our mozzarella with Albino Scalizzitti, an artisan cheesemaker from the Molise region. We sourced ingredients locally and trained *pizzaioli* to master the ancient art of the Neapolitan oven. Our aim was to restore the reputation of the wonderful product that is pizza, and mend the injured "mouth" of the consumer. Most people encouraged us. Others were skeptical, telling us that "the public will not understand the difference." Fortunately for us, they did.

This book has exactly the same ethos as the Franco Manca restaurants and, like them, is an attempt to snatch pizzas from the jaws of globalization. We want to encourage you to go back to the stove and the oven. The first and main principle is simple: know your products, your sources, and what you are eating.

Engage, knead, think, bake, and enjoy!

ESSENTIALS

- - - - - - - - - - - - - - - - - -

Before you start, there are a few things you need to consider, and a few things you may need to buy. Whereas recipes are like still images of a moving life—always an incomplete means to convey what one has in mind—many cooking basics can be measured as objects or used as rules.

Our main aim is to inspire and help, not to dictate. Our descriptions are preliminary indications, and your own close encounters will fill out a much larger, personal picture.

In this section you will find a few keys. Which doors they unlock, or rooms they reveal, remains to be seen!

EQUIPMENT

BOWL

Our dough recipes feed four and make under 2 pounds of dough, so a 2-quart ceramic bowl is perfect.

Traditionally, pizza dough was mixed in a *madia*, a rectangular, hardwood container, usually made of beechwood.

ROLLING PIN

Pizzas are traditionally stretched by hand, but if you are inexperienced you may prefer to use a rolling pin. The best ones have no handles and are made of a hardwood, such as pear or cherry, but they always need to be 16 to 20 inches long and 2 to 3 inches in diameter. The wood has to be very well seasoned or it will warp.

SCALES

Using scales is highly recommended, especially for making dough, when all your measurements need to be precise, but especially your liquid ones (i.e. water). The best are balancing scales, since they do not break and do not require electricity. Digital scales are good, too.

CONTAINERS

While rising, dough balls are usually stored in beechwood boxes 2 to 3 inches deep. You can make one for yourself to fit your fridge. You can also buy professional plastic pizza boxes, but even the smallest of these is quite large.

Hardwood is best, since good pizza dough is very hydrated and the wood helps absorb moisture from the dough balls, which sweat as they develop.

Plastic is not as good but, if your container has a lid, provides decent insulation. The easiest alternative is a deep baking sheet, although it offers poor insulation. If you go for this option, it is important to cover the balls with a damp cloth or thin towel. Tuck it under the baking sheet to create a bit of tension so the cloth does not collapse onto the dough balls and stick. If you use plastic wrap, brush it with oil first.

PIZZA STONE

In our experience, most domestic ovens fail to reach a sufficiently high temperature to make using a pizza stone worthwhile–it rarely becomes hot enough. This is not to say you should not try it. If you use a stone, you will also need a peel (a long-handled, spadelike tool) to move the pizza in and out of the oven.

CAST–IRON PAN

The baked pizzas in this book are all made using a cast-iron pan. The dough is started on the stove and then, after the toppings are added, it is moved inside the oven or under a broiler to finish. A suitable cast-iron pan–10 inches in diameter–is easy to come by, not expensive, and will last a lifetime. However, even this simple piece of equipment needs maintaining, so always dry it thoroughly after cleaning and oil it immediately, or it will rust. If it does start to rust, place it on the heat and rub it with oiled paper towels until the rust is removed.

If you already have a pan but of a different size, you can adapt the size of your dough balls to fit–here's another good argument for having scales!

BAKING SHEET

The dough recipe for baking sheet pizza fits either a regular-sized baking sheet (11 × 16 inches), or two smaller baking sheets (7 × 12 inches). They do not need to be nonstick since you oil them anyway before baking.

DEEP FRYER

Pizza can be fried in a deep pot or in a deep fryer if you have one.

THERMOMETER

A household or catering thermometer is essential for the novice pizzamaker, as we'll explain in the instructions for making dough. If you are deep-frying, an immersion thermometer is also useful.

DOUGH SCRAPER

This has either a plastic or wooden handle and a sharp metal edge. It's used not only to cut the dough and scrape clean the pizza sheet, but also to lift the balls out of the dough tray.

SPOONS

A large metal spoon will help you to measure the sauce as well as spread it onto the pizza. Other standard measuring spoons and cups will also come in handy.

DOUGH

There is no secret to a dough recipe—it is flour, water, and salt... and yet each of these elements is key.

WATER

Water and flour have a vital relationship, and the amount of water you need in the mix depends on the type of flour you use. A "strong" bread flour absorbs more water and results in a stiff dough that makes for a hard and crispy crust. If you want a chewy dough with a lighter crust, it is best to use more water with a "weaker" flour, like all-purpose flour, which will give you a more elastic dough.

FLOUR

The best is always stone-milled and made by humans rather than machines. It needs to be stored somewhere neither too wet nor too dry and, ideally, should be used within 6 months.

We use bread flour for our basic recipe. Stone-milled is preferable, but the really important thing is that it has not been bleached since this means it is free of chemicals, more nutritious, and superior in taste. In Italy and France, flours are classified by their ash content, which means the amount of bran (the outer layer of the kernel of wheat) left after the milling process. Classification starts with the highest content (whole-wheat = 2) going down to 1, 0, and 00. The best flour for pizza is 1 or 0 (although you could use a 2 if you want a more whole-wheat taste and a 00 for a very white pizza).

Stone-milled flour is the best for making pizza at home and tends to be either 1 or 0, even when described as a white bread flour. It will generally have an ash content of between 0.60 and 0.80%.

Protein (or gluten) is also key, as this is what gives the dough good elasticity and robustness. The ideal content is about 12 to 13% and you can blend two flours (say a bread flour that is 15% with an all-purpose flour that is 9% protein) to get the ideal 50:50 blend.

SALT

Salt is not simply a matter of taste. It has its own chemical attributes and will affect the absorption of water and also the bacterial action in sourdough recipes. In general, salt content in pizza recipes ranges from ¾ ounce to 1½ ounces per 2 pounds of flour used, depending on the toppings.

The pizzerias in Naples that serve only Margherita and Marinara tend to use a lot of salt in their dough and no salt in their topping to enhance the flavor of the pizza. (Tomato sauce also keeps better if it has no salt in it.) But for a Pepperoni pizza, you would use less salt in the dough to balance the salty sausage. In this book, as a rule of thumb, we use ¾ ounce (½ tablespoon) of salt per pound of flour.

YEAST

Fresh and dry yeast are fairly interchangeable. Dry yeast is easier to come by and easier to use, so we use this in our recipes here. However, many people love the smell of fresh yeast as it activates and if this is your preferred method, go right ahead. You will need 1 ounce of fresh yeast for every ⅓ ounce of dry when substituting.

SOURDOUGH STARTER

This is a "living food" of flour and water that contains yeast-producing bacteria collected from the air. The result is a culture, similar to yogurt (although the bacteria are of a different sort). Once you have the right bacteria, continue to feed the colony with flour and water.

These days, many people enjoy the practice of starting and maintaining a sourdough culture and, although an ongoing activity (a little like having a pet), a relationship develops, which makes the responsibility worthwhile.

In southern Italy the starter (*crescito* or *levata*) is often passed around a small village as one family will bake on Saturday and another midweek.

FERMENTATION

The length of the fermentation is more relevant than whether you are making a yeast or sourdough pizza. A long fermentation will transform the starch into noble sugars and work through the proteins, making a much more digestible and better tasting pizza. It does mean preparing the dough roughly 24 hours in advance but you can make a batch of dough to freeze for future use. If doing this, follow the dough recipe for baked pizzas right up until the product is shaped, and then freeze the bases.

TEMPERATURE

Temperature is very important when making pizza dough as ideally, the water, flour, and ambient temperature should all be 64 to 68°F. In the absence of a thermometer, your aim is for water to be warm to the touch, but not at all hot. If your room temperature is very hot, you can use cold water. If very cold, you will need to use warm water and add a little more yeast or starter to the recipe–but no more than 30% more.

PROPORTIONS

At Franco Manca we make a very hydrated dough that, when baked in the extreme heat of traditional, wood-fired brick ovens, produces a juicy pizza with a crust textured with air bubbles and puffed up–the proverbial Neapolitan *cornicione*. However, we understand that making pizza in a home kitchen is different and therefore we have adapted our recipe so you can achieve the best results in that setting.

The recipes here make a dough that is moist and flexible but not too difficult to handle. The aim is to use as much water as possible but if you find the dough unmanageable, slightly reduce the quantity of water.

FRANCO MANCA SOURDOUGH

At Franco Manca we use only sourdough because it adds an extra dimension to the taste. For the same reason, we always give it a long 24-hour fermentation. This method ensures good texture, great taste and added nutritional values.

THE FOLLOWING DOUGH RECIPES MAKE ROUGHLY ENOUGH TO FEED FOUR, EITHER FOUR PIZZAS BAKED IN A PAN, OR ONE SHEET PIZZA (ENOUGH TO FEED FOUR). IF YOU WANT TO MAKE LARGER PIZZAS (USING A PEEL AND A PIZZA STONE) OR IF YOU HAVE MORE MOUTHS TO FEED, SIMPLY INCREASE THE QUANTITY OF DOUGH.

DOUGH I

FOR BAKED & FRIED PIZZAS

This dough will take about 16 to 18 hours to develop, so it is ideal to make it in the late evening for an early supper the following night. You can also make the dough in the morning for use in the evening by adding 20% more yeast. When working in this slow, natural timeframe, surprisingly little yeast is required (see tip opposite). Once you have made the recipe and you remember how much yeast you "measured," it may be simpler to use just a pinch.

This is assuming you leave the dough in an ambient temperature of 68 to 73°F. If the temperature is colder (59 to 64°F) it will take a few hours longer.

YEAST VERSION

MAKES 1½ POUNDS
1 cup lukewarm (70°F) water
0.01 ounce dry yeast
1 teaspoon olive oil
3 cups (13 ounces) flour
½ tablespoon salt

SOURDOUGH VERSION

MAKES 1½ POUNDS
1 cup lukewarm (70°F) water
1 ounce starter
½ tablespoon olive oil
3 cups (13 ounces) flour
½ tablespoon salt

I. Pour the water into a bowl, and add the yeast (or sourdough starter). Stir or whisk in, then add the olive oil.

2 Place the flour and salt in a large, 2-quart ceramic bowl and combine the ingredients with your fingertips.

3. Pour the liquid into the flour in a few stages, mixing each time with stiff fingers. (Note: use your left hand for pouring water if you are right-handed.)

4. Work lightly, using only your fingers to draw the dough together and mop up all the flour. Avoid getting dough on the palm of your hand. Knead the dough a little with your knuckles.

5. Once the ingredients have roughly combined, you can rest the dough. This gives the flour time to absorb the water and will make the dough easier to knead.

6. After 15 minutes, use your fingers and knuckles to knead the dough for about 5 minutes. Dipping your fingers in water will help keep the dough from sticking to your fingers while you do this.

7. Once kneaded, cover the bowl with plastic wrap or a damp cloth and leave the dough to sit for 1 hour.

8. With a lightly oiled hand this time, fold the dough by drawing the four edges consecutively into the center and then pressing down on them. With the shape of your hands, form a large ball and then turn the mass over. Brush a bit more olive oil on top and cover the bowl again to store, making sure it's airtight.

9. Leave the dough in an ambient temperature of 68 to 73°F and in 16–18 hours, your dough will be ready to use. If the temperature is colder (59 to 64°F) it will take a little longer.

TIP

Dividing the yeast can seem tricky, but it is not so. Usually a packet of dry yeast is ¼ ounce. Divide this in half on a smooth surface using a plastic card or dough scraper five times.

SHAPING BALLS

The baked and fried pizzas both start with a ball of dough that is opened (stretched) into shape: For pan baking, 5 to 6 ounce balls will fit easily into the base of a 10-inch cast-iron pan. For *pizzette* (small, fried pizzas), cut the dough into 2-ounce balls.

I. Transfer the dough onto a floured surface and divide the developed dough mass into equal pieces with a dough cutter. For our dough recipe, divide it by 4. Alternatively, you can weigh your balls on your scale.

2. Knock back the dough pieces by rolling them in a circle on a table until they form tight balls. When you do this, keep a tight grip around the edges of the ball with your fingertips while applying some pressure from the palm of your hand on top. You may want to practice, but do not overdo the shaping of each ball, as you will stress and tear the dough.

3. Place these on a floured surface in an airtight container or in a deep baking sheet. If using a baking sheet, drape a dampened kitchen towel over it, but be sure to tuck the edges of the cloth under the sheet, so the rising dough does not stick to the sagging cloth. In a cool kitchen (64°F), these balls will take up to 2 hours to rise. In a warm kitchen (75°F), 1 hour will be enough.

BAKING IN A CAST—IRON PAN

1. Rub a 10-inch cast-iron pan with a little olive oil and place it on the stove to get hot.

2. Sprinkle a little flour on your hands and on the table. Open a dough ball by flattening and stretching the dough gently with your fingers, or by rolling the dough with a rolling pin.

3. Pick the pizza base up and gently, without tearing, stretch it a little further over your fists. Transfer the shaped pizza onto the hot pan.

4. Once the pizza starts to bubble and turn golden underneath, it will be stiff enough to add toppings. After 3 to 4 minutes, transfer the pan to a 475°F oven (with the door shut) or place under a hot broiler to finish. We find using a broiler gives foolproof results.

FRYING

1. Divide the dough into 8 or 16 pieces. Shape these into round balls, cover, and leave to rise for at least an hour in a warm place.

2. In a wide saucepan, warm ¾ cup peanut oil (best) or vegetable oil (never olive oil) over medium heat to reach a temperature of no more than 350°F (if you have a probe thermometer, this will be helpful).

3. Place a dough ball on a floured surface next to the stove. With your fingertips, flatten the ball into a disk, then pick this up and stretch it out a little, before placing in the hot oil.

4. Cook each pizzetta for a minute or so, then turn over. Do not overcook—if fried to a dark brown, the flavor will be impaired. Place on paper towels to soak up the oil and then add toppings while warm.

STONE BAKING

We definitely prefer the pan-baking method since if your oven is not hot enough or the stone you are using is not the best, the dough doesn't cook thoroughly underneath or rise enough on the stone. However, it is worth trying, and with a little experimenting, you can achieve satisfaction. Here's the method to try.

1. Turn the oven on to its highest setting and place a pizza stone on the highest rack to heat for at least 15 minutes after the oven has reached full temperature.

2. Sprinkle a little flour on the peel (see page 11) and open the dough ball onto it.

3. Follow the recipes for baked pizzas from the pages ahead. Using a peel, move the prepared pizza onto the stone and bake for about 8 to 10 minutes.

DOUGH 2

FOR SHEET-BAKED PIZZAS

The best baking sheet pizzas are made with a very wet and elastic dough, based on a method using "poolish" (an equal mix of flour and water with added yeast). This is made about 16 hours in advance of the dough. The total dough recipe here makes enough for one pizza (2 pounds) and is enough to feed four.

The best way to mix this dough is to use an electric mixer with a dough hook. If working without, be prepared to apply elbow grease.

FOR THE POOLISH	FOR THE DOUGH
1^2/$_3$ cups lukewarm (72°F) water	1^1/$_4$ cups (5^2/$_3$ ounces) flour
3^1/$_4$ cups (14 oz) flour	^{1}/$_2$ tablespoon dry yeast
^{1}/$_2$ tablespoon dry yeast	1 tablespoon sugar
	^{3}/$_4$ tablespoon salt
	2 tablespoons olive oil

NOTE: Make the poolish the day before you make pizza by combining all the ingredients in a bowl. Cover and set aside in the fridge for AT LEAST 16 hours and no longer than 48 hours.

1. In a large bowl, mix the flour, yeast, and sugar into the poolish and combine. As it comes together, use the strength of your arm and stiff fingers to beat it for about 6 minutes. You might have to rest every few minutes! With a mixer this should take about 4 minutes. You are aiming for a smooth, elastic dough that starts to "shine."

2. Add the salt and oil and mix again until these ingredients are absorbed into the dough, then turn the mixture out into a lightly oiled bowl and rest for 20 minutes.

3. Transfer the dough onto an oiled baking sheet and fold into shape, following the dimensions of the sheet you're using. Then turn it over, so the "good" side is up.

4. Turn your oven on at its highest setting and place a rack on the middle shelf.

5. Stretch the dough toward the edges of the sheet in two stages, resting for 10 minutes between each stretch. When stretching the dough, try not to touch it on top, but use your finger tips from underneath the dough mass.

6. After the second stretch, add your toppings. If using tomato sauce, make sure it is spread right to the edges of the dough. If you are using olive oil, pour it into the palm of your hands and pat it lightly over the top of the dough, again making sure it touches the edges.

7. If the dough is deep (or the sheet small) you can dimple the dough with your fingertips, making a focaccia-style deep pizza and adding more sauce or oil. If you have stretched the dough very thin, simply add the rest of your ingredients and seasonings.

8. Bake on the middle rack of your preheated oven for 12 to 14 minutes. If you have created a very thin pizza base, check for doneness after 10 minutes.

TOMATO

Good-quality tomatoes are key to a rich-tasting pizza sauce so try to source the best you can find. Fresh tomatoes have a short season in summer, anything between 6 weeks in temperate zones to 3 months in warmer climes. For the rest of the year, unless you've made your own passata, which we highly recommend, you are better off buying canned tomatoes.

PASSATA

When the best fresh tomatoes are used for passata, no additional cooking is needed, and the sauce can be used as is. Depending your tomatoes' juiciness, different quantities of passata will be yielded. You should get about 1 quart of passata from every 11 pounds of tomatoes.

a large shopping bag of San Marzano or plum tomatoes

a few basil leaves, torn

I. Sort through the tomatoes, cutting off any black parts and discarding any that are damaged. Wash well and soak in boiled water for 2 to 3 minutes, then drain in a colander.

2. Pass the tomatoes through a food mill, collecting the pulp, which is now ready to be bottled. Add a leaf of basil for extra flavor. Use sealable bottles (for example, beer bottles with a crown) or jars with lids, and sterilize them before jarring the passata.

3. To sterilize the jars of passata again once they're full, cover them, place them in a deep pan, and fill the pan with cold water, almost to the rims of the jars. Bring to a boil, then remove the pan from the heat. If you have a thermometer, you can take the pot off the heat when the water has reached 195°F.

4. Your passata will keep for a year if stored in a cool, dark place.

BASIC SALSA

Without fresh tomatoes, you can make an on-the-spot sauce using either bought tomato sauce or canned tomatoes. (Italian products tend to be better.) When buying cans, go for whole, peeled tomatoes instead of chopped, because they're better quality. The sauce will develop extra flavor if you reduce it slightly and add a little basil. We recommend you add garlic or chile only to your pizzas (not to your sauce) since they do not complement all toppings, particularly in their raw state.

MAKES ENOUGH FOR 4 PIZZAS

1 small can whole, peeled tomatoes

fine sea salt, to taste
fresh basil, torn

I. In a large bowl, squeeze the tomatoes hard through your fingers to crush.

2. If you are reducing your sauce, simmer in a pan over low heat for 5 minutes.

3. Add a few leaves of fresh basil and fine sea salt to taste. The flavor should all be in the tomatoes so be careful not to oversalt.

SALSA LARDIATA (CON SUGNA)

If you are after a richer tomato topping, this is a great variation you can use for both the passata and basic salsa. Either regular lard or a speciality cured lard (see page 71) will add flavor to the meaty tang of the reduced tomatoes, and the onion keeps the deal sweet.

MAKES 2 CUPS

2 cups passata or fresh,
    juicy tomatoes peeled
    and chopped
1 1/2 oz lard or cured lard

1 medium onion
sea salt and freshly
    ground black
    pepper, to taste

1. On a chopping board, with heavy knife, chop the onion together with the lard, beating the lard into the onion with the blunt edge of the knife.

2. In a frying pan, season the onion and cook gently over low heat until the onion has "melted."

3. Add the tomato, stir to combine, and leave to simmer for at least 1 hour (the longer the better). Season to taste, being careful not to oversalt.

CHEESE

There are many ways to make pizzas without tomato, but few can imagine pizza without cheese, and mozzarella in particular. The other Italian cheeses used on pizza are ricotta, provolone, and caciocavallo. However, there are many other cheeses you can try and, in recent years, there has been a great resurgence of artisanal cheeses. There are a number of amazing artisanal cheeses, and at Franco Manca we make use many of them.

Mozzarella

Mozzarella used for cooking is always *fior di latte*, or cow's milk mozzarella. Buffalo mozzarella is only ever added on top of a pizza after it has been baked. Proper *fior di latte* has either no or low pasteurization, which means it will last no more than 3 days. Increasingly, small cheesemakers outside Italy are making their own mozzarella. You can even buy a kit to make it yourself. At Franco Manca, we've trained a cheesemaker in Somerset to make our mozzarella and also ricotta.

Ricotta

The better varieties of ricotta are firm and fairly dry, and we suggest thinning them slightly with milk, to make *crema di ricotta*. Store-bought ricotta is usually already fairly soft.

Parmesan

If you are using Parmesan, use only Reggiano. Other Parmesans might cost less but are often tasteless and have a waxy texture.

Roquefort

If you need a blue cheese, you can never go wrong with Roquefort. Most countries, though, have their

own varieties, so always experiment. The best will be the cheese one has found from a farmer one has met, if possible. As with all things in life, we are biased toward people we know, and rightly so.

Gruyère

Another variety of cheese good for some recipes is a Comté or Gruyère (Comté used to be Gruyère and, despite leaving the appelation, it still is). Of the Swiss and French Gruyères, the French is said to have less bite.

SMOKING YOUR OWN CHEESE

Smoked mozzarella adds a wonderful dimension to certain pizzas and we've included recipes on page 45, 65, 66, 88, 105 and 121. It's very easy to smoke your own, and you don't even need a proper smoker. Here's the method for making tea or straw-smoked mozzarella.

1 x 4 to 5 ounce
    mozzarella ball
1 teaspoon loose-leaf
    tea (preferably white
    or silver tea) or straw

I. Remove the mozzarella from its packaging, pat dry with paper towels, and rest in the fridge for 12 to 24 hours until it dries out (it must be dry enough not to drip).

2. If you have a smoker, cold-smoke for 10 minutes with either tea or straw. If you don't have a smoker, place the mozzarella on a piece of wire mesh and place this in the oven on the top rack.

3. Scatter the tea or straw onto a baking sheet and cover with foil, ensuring all the edges are sealed. If there are any tears, start again, or your smoke will escape.

4. Place the baking sheet on the stove and heat until it is very hot. This will trap a lot of smoke.

5. Carefully transfer the baking sheet to the oven, remove the foil and immediately shut the oven door. Repeat the operation after 15 minutes, then leave the cheese for 20 minutes in the oven.

OILS & FATS

Oils and fats add an extra layer of flavor to pizzas, as do animal drippings. Olive oil is the traditional oil used, and the best is made from olives that are not only free from insecticides and cold pressed, but also hand-picked. You can flavor olive oil very effectively with garlic, chile, or herbs (see page 58), and this makes both a wonderful pizza ingredient or optional condiment.

It is not necessary, though, to limit yourself to olive oil. Some of the best pizzerias in Naples use other vegetable oils–Pizzeria Michele uses soy oil. You could also use cold-pressed canola oil, which has a wonderful color, although it lacks the flavor of olive oil. Peanut oil is also good.

If you roast a duck or goose you will end up with copious amounts of delicious fat. The same applies to pork fat. Many Neapolitan *pizzaioli* use the latter as a "secret" ingredient to enhance the taste of their pizzas.

RENDERING LARD

This quantity of back fat will give you about 3 pounds of lard. After you have fried the fat, you will be left with soft pork scratchings. Mix these with some salt and freshly ground black pepper and either vacuum-pack or refrigerate in a sealed container.

4½ pounds pork back
    fat, separated from
    the rind and cut into
    small cubes

I. Place the fat in a pan, cover with water, and bring to a very low boil. Leave to simmer on very low heat. As the water evaporates, the fat will start to melt. Do not allow the fat to color.

2. When all the fat has melted and is still very hot, carefully drain through a sieve and pour into sterilized glass jars. Seal and store either in the fridge or a cool, dark place for up to 6 months.

PIZZAS

The recipes that follow show quantities per pizza, so multiply these by the number of people you plan to enjoy your pizzas with. The dough recipes are already calculated to make enough for four people, because it is not worth making less dough than this at a time.

Quality ingredients are important and the prep does require a certain amount of time—maintaining your sourdough starter and waiting for the fermentation of dough, for example—yet pizza making will still feel like a spontaneous and joyful event when it comes to the final baking.

The selection of toppings and the preparation of some of these also requires a little forethought, but any time spent seeking out the best ingredients will bring rewards that utterly justify your efforts.

The Margherita is a benchmark pizza and provides the ultimate taste test for your raw materials of dough, tomato, olive oil, and cheese. Make sure they're the best and you can't go wrong. Use this recipe to test your skills and the quality of your principal ingredients before venturing into the wonderful world of other toppings.

MARGHERITA BAKED OR SHEET

ingredients, per pizza

1 dough ball (see page 16), left to rise for 1½ to 2 hours OR dough 2 for sheet pizzas

flour, for dusting

1 teaspoon tomato sauce (see page 20)

2 teaspoons olive oil

2 ounces *mozzarella fior di latte*, torn into 5 chunks

4 basil leaves, torn, plus more to serve

Place a rack on the highest shelf of the oven and turn the broiler to its highest setting. When hot, place a greased 10-inch cast-iron pan on the stove, set to medium heat.

Sprinkle a little flour over your hands and on the work surface and open the dough ball by flattening and stretching the dough with your fingers, or by rolling the dough with a rolling pin. Pick the pizza base up and gently stretch it a little more over your fists without tearing it. Drop this onto the hot pan and allow it to start rising.

As soon as the dough firms up, spread the tomato sauce over the base with the back of a metal spoon. Drizzle with olive oil and distribute the basil and mozzarella on top.

Cook the pizza on top of the stove for about 3 minutes, then transfer the pan to the broiler for another 3 to 4 minutes.

Once ready, decorate with a little more basil and serve in one piece or sliced.

For the sheet method

Follow the recipe instructions on page 19. The whole process will take about 90 minutes. Heat the oven to 500°F and stretch the dough to the edges of the baking sheet. Be sure to spread your sauce right to the edges before adding toppings. The sheet pizza dough serves 4, so quadruple the ingredient quantities. Bake for no less than 10 minutes.

> *INGREDIENT NOTE*
> ----------------
> A Margherita sometimes has a very small quantity of *crotonese* (a sheep's cheese from Calabria), which has a very strong but rounded taste. Another way to enhance the flavor, used by master *pizzaioli*, is to add a tablespoon of lard.

This is a bianca pizza—meaning the base is white (*bianco*), i.e. without a tomato sauce. Here, the base simply forms the bread accompaniment to what is essentially a cured meat and cheese salad. With such fresh ingredients, this is perfect for summer, served with drizzles of good olive oil.

BRESAOLA, CHERRY TOMATOES, & BUFFALO MOZZARELLA BAKED

ingredients, per pizza

1 dough ball (see page 16), left to rise for 1½ to 2 hours

flour, for dusting

2 teaspoons extra virgin olive oil

5 cherry tomatoes, halved

a handful of arugula, washed

2 ounces buffalo mozzarella, torn into 5 chunks

4 slices bresaola

freshly ground black pepper

Place a rack on the highest shelf of the oven and turn the broiler to its highest setting. When hot, place a greased 10-inch cast-iron pan on the stove, set to medium heat.

Sprinkle a little flour over your hands and on the work surface and open the dough ball by flattening and stretching the dough with your fingers, or by rolling the dough with a rolling pin. Pick the pizza base up and gently stretch it a little more over your fists without tearing it. Drop this onto the hot pan, and allow it to start rising.

As soon as the dough firms up, drizzle the olive oil over the base. Cook the pizza on top of the stove for about 3 minutes, then transfer the pan to the broiler for another 3 to 4 minutes.

Once ready, dress with all the ingredients in the order listed and finish with a couple of grinds of fresh black pepper.

INGREDIENT NOTE

See page 71 for how to make your own bresaola. It also makes a great antipasto, simply dressed with a squeeze of lemon, a drizzle of olive oil, and a few grinds of black pepper. Slice as thinly as possible.

Good pancetta is essential to this recipe so it might require a trip to your local butcher or deli (and ask for it to be sliced thinly). If you only have an average bacon, we recommend you use good-quality cooked ham instead.

PANCETTA & EGGPLANT BAKED

ingredients, per pizza

1 dough ball (see page 16),
    left to rise for
    1^1/$_2$ to 2 hours
flour, for dusting

5 thin slices eggplant
1 tablespoon extra virgin
    olive oil
sea salt
2 tablespoons tomato
    sauce (see page 20)
4 slices pancetta
2 ounces *mozzarella fior di
    latte*, torn into 5 chunks
4 basil leaves, torn
a handful of arugula
Parmesan, grated
    (optional)

Place a rack on the highest shelf of the oven and turn the broiler to its highest setting. When hot, place a greased 10-inch cast-iron pan on the stove, set to medium heat.

In a shallow pan, cook the eggplant in 2 teaspoons olive oil until soft, golden, and a little crispy. Season with salt to taste and set aside.

Sprinkle a little flour over your hands and on the work surface and open the dough ball by flattening and stretching the dough with your fingers, or by rolling the dough with a rolling pin. Pick the pizza base up and gently stretch it a little more over your fists without tearing it. Drop this onto the hot pan, and allow it to start rising.

As the dough firms up, spread the tomato sauce evenly over the base with the back of a metal spoon. Add the pancetta and eggplant, then drizzle with the remaining olive oil and scatter the mozzarella and basil.

Cook the pizza on top of the stove for about 3 minutes, then transfer the pan to the broiler for another 3 to 4 minutes.

Once ready, dress with the arugula leaves, and a little grated Parmesan won't hurt either, if you have it. Serve whole or in slices.

This simple pizza makes use of the softest mozzarella—"burratina"—that takes the taste to such a distinct level of creaminess that it is best eaten uncooked. This simple topping is also great for small, fried pizzette (see page 116).

BURRATA PUGLIESE   *BAKED OR FRIED*

ingredients, per pizza

1 dough ball (see page 16),
   left to rise for
   1½ to 2 hours
flour, for dusting

2 teaspoons extra virgin
   olive oil
5 cherry tomatoes, halved
3 ounces burratina, torn
   into 6 chunks
a handful of arugula,
   washed
freshly ground black
   pepper

Place a rack on the highest shelf of the oven and turn the broiler to its highest setting. When hot, place a greased 10-inch cast-iron pan on the stove, set to medium heat.

Sprinkle a little flour over your hands and on the work surface and open the dough ball by flattening and stretching the dough with your fingers, or by rolling the dough with a rolling pin. Pick the pizza base up and gently stretch it a little more over your fists without tearing it. Drop this onto the hot pan, and allow it to start rising.

As soon as the dough firms up, drizzle the olive oil over the base. Cook the pizza on top of the stove for about 3 minutes, then transfer the pan to the broiler for another 3 to 4 minutes.

Dress with all the ingredients in the order above, and finish with a couple of grinds of fresh black pepper.

For fried pizza, see the method on page 17

Pesto and potato are a common pairing in Italy since they are made from readily available garden ingredients. In fact, Genovese pasta recipes for pesto also usually include cooked potato. The garlic and herbs marry well with the creamy potatoes, and the result is hearty yet simple.

PESTO WITH BAKED POTATO & PARMESAN BAKED

ingredients, per pizza

1 dough ball (see page 16),
   left to rise for
   1½ to 2 hours
flour, for dusting

for the potato topping
   (makes enough
   for 4 baked pizzas)

11 ounces potatoes,
   washed and cut into
   small wedges
3 teaspoons olive oil
1 teaspoon fine sea salt
½ medium onion,
   finely sliced
½ cup cherry tomatoes,
   halved

1 tablespoon tomato sauce
   (see page 20)
3 teaspoons basil pesto
   (see page 34)
2 ounces *mozzarella fior di latte*, torn into 5 chunks
Parmesan shavings
2 teaspoons extra virgin
   olive oil

Make the potato topping: Preheat the oven to 400°F.

In a roasting pan, mix the potatoes with 2 teaspoons of olive oil and sea salt, and bake in the oven for about 40 minutes. Drain on paper towels.

In a heavy pan, sweat the onions in 1 teaspoon of oil over very low heat until soft. Turn up the heat slightly and add the cherry tomatoes to the pan. When the ingredients start to caramelize and become sticky, add the baked potato wedges and turn off the heat. While the mixture cools, toss well.

Place a rack on the highest shelf of the oven and turn the broiler to its highest setting. When hot, place a greased 10-inch cast-iron pan on the stove, set to medium heat.

Sprinkle a little flour over your hands and on the work surface and open the dough ball by flattening and stretching the dough with your fingers, or by rolling the dough with a rolling pin. Pick the pizza base up and gently stretch it a little more over your fists without tearing it. Drop this onto the hot pan, and allow it to start rising.

As soon as the dough firms up, spread the tomato sauce over the base with the back of a metal spoon. Distribute a quarter of the baked potato mixture on top and finish with the basil pesto and mozzarella.

Cook the pizza on top of the stove for about 3 minutes, then transfer the pan to the broiler for another 3 to 4 minutes.

Dress with the shaved Parmesan and a little more oil and serve in pieces or whole.

BASIL PESTO

PESTO DI BASILICO

Pesto is traditionally made with a mortar and pestle—ideally a stone mortar and a wooden pestle.

If you use a food processor, blend in the same order as given below. Genovese pesto has about half the quantity of oil given in this recipe but is specifically for use with pasta. You can use Neapolitan, large-leaf basil with a bit of Greek basil, if you like.

MAKES 1 CUP

2 to 3 garlic cloves
1 teaspoon coarse sea salt
2 ounces basil leaves
1 tablespoon pine nuts or chopped walnuts
1 cup olive oil
$1/3$ cup Pecorino (or aged sheep's cheese), grated
$3/4$ cup Parmigiano reggiano, grated

With a mortar and pestle, crush the garlic with half the salt. When well crushed, add the basil and the remaining salt. Rotating the pestle against the side of the mortar, keep crushing the pesto until the basil releases a green liquid. Add the pine nuts and keep crushing. (If you use walnuts, use ones in the shell, as the shelled walnuts degenerate easily, acquiring a rancid aftertaste.)

When all is well crushed, start adding the oil and the cheeses until you have an homogenous mix.

WILD GARLIC PESTO

AGLIO SELVATICO PESTO

In spring, you should be able to find plenty of garlic growing in the wild. However, it is also possible to cultivate some in a shady corner of your garden. This pesto is a wonderful way to enjoy it.

MAKES 200ML

2 to 3 garlic cloves
$2^{1}/2$ cups wild garlic greens (ramps)
$2/3$ cup olive oil
$3/4$ cup grated aged Cheddar or sheep cheese

Blend everything together, starting with the garlic and wild garlic greens and finishing with the cheese and the oil—either in a mortar and pestle or in a blender.

Good lamb makes a great alternative to cooked ham or cured meat as a pizza topping and combines well with a hard cheese like Pecorino. We find that children and anyone who is impartial to mozzarella are particularly fond of this pizza.

GROUND LAMB & PECORINO BAKED OR SHEET

ingredients, per pizza

1 dough ball (see page 16),
  left to rise for
  1½ to 2 hours OR
  dough 2 for sheet pizzas
flour, for dusting

2½ tablespoons tomato
  sauce (see page 20)
2 teaspoons extra virgin
  olive oil
2 to 3 ounces ground lamb
  (see below)
2 ounces *mozzarella fior di
  latte*, torn into 5 chunks
4 basil leaves, torn
4 teaspoons Pecorino

for the ground lamb
  (makes enough
  for 4 baked pizzas)
1 tablespoon olive oil
10 ounces ground lamb
1 teaspoon fine sea salt
1 garlic clove, peeled and
  crushed
a few mint leaves, finely
  chopped
2 teaspoons grated
  Pecorino

Make the lamb: Heat the oil in a wide, shallow pan over medium heat, then add all the ingredients and cook briefly until the lamb turns slightly brown. (It will cook more thoroughly and crisp slightly once on the pizza.)

Place a rack on the highest shelf of the oven and turn the broiler to its highest setting. When hot, place a greased 10-inch cast-iron pan on the stove, set to medium heat.

Sprinkle a little flour over your hands and on the work surface and open the dough ball by flattening and stretching the dough with your fingers, or by rolling the dough with a rolling pin. Pick the pizza base up and gently stretch it a little more over your fists without tearing it. Drop this onto the hot pan, and allow it to start rising.

As soon as the dough firms up, spread the tomato sauce over the base with the back of a metal spoon and drizzle the olive oil on top. Crumble a quarter of the lamb over the pizza and then finish with the mozzarella, basil, and Pecorino.

Cook the pizza on top of the stove for about 3 minutes, then transfer the pan to the broiler for another 3 to 4 minutes.

Serve whole or in slices.

For the sheet method
Follow the recipe instructions on page 19. The whole process will take about 90 minutes. Heat the oven to 500°F and stretch the dough to the edges of the baking sheet. Be sure to spread your sauce right to the edges before adding toppings. The sheet pizza dough serves four, so quadruple the ingredient quantities. Bake for no less than 10 minutes.

INGREDIENT NOTE.
- - - - - - - - - - - - - - - -
The lamb here and the recipe for spicy lamb (see page 60) can both also be used for the meatball pizza (see page 46). Either prepare in advance or after you have shaped the balls, while the dough is rising.

Many people believe the Marinara is a seafood pizza—it is not, but rather a simple vegan pizza that includes no meat or cheese. The name refers to a sailor's wife, *La Marinara*, who might be expected to offer her returning husband something simple and unfussy to eat.

MARINARA BAKED

ingredients, per pizza

1 dough ball (see page 16),
   left to rise for
   1½ to 2 hours
flour, for dusting

1 tablespoon plus
   1 teaspoon olive oil
1 garlic clove, peeled and
   roughly chopped
1 tablespoon tomato sauce
   (see page 20)
½ teaspoon dried oregano
4 basil leaves, torn
sea salt and freshly ground
   black pepper

Place a rack on the highest shelf of the oven and turn the broiler to its highest setting. When hot, place a greased 10-inch cast-iron pan on the stove, set to medium heat.

In a saucepan, heat half the olive oil on low heat and cook the garlic until lightly golden. Stir in the tomato sauce and set aside.

Sprinkle a little flour over your hands and on the work surface and open the dough ball by flattening and stretching the dough with your fingers, or by rolling the dough with a rolling pin. Pick the pizza base up and gently stretch it a little more over your fists without tearing it. Drop this onto the hot pan, and allow it to start rising.

As soon as the dough firms, spread the tomato and garlic sauce over the base with the back of a metal spoon. Drizzle with the remaining olive oil and finish with the oregano.

Cook the pizza on top of the stove for about 3 minutes, then transfer the pan to the broiler for another 3 to 4 minutes.

Once ready, garnish with fresh basil, season to taste, and serve in one piece or sliced.

Cooked ham and mushrooms make a very popular pizza topping, probably because both are fairly moist, with gentle flavors and textures. Good ricotta can also be described in these terms, which is why it is used here to complete the ingredient trilogy.

HAM, MUSHROOM, & RICOTTA   BAKED

ingredients, per pizza

1 dough ball (see page 16),
    left to rise for
    1½ to 2 hours
flour, for dusting

for the *crema di ricotta*
    (makes enough
    for 1 baked pizza)
2 teaspoons milk
1 heaping tablespoon
    ricotta
sea salt and freshly ground
    black pepper

for the wild mushrooms
    (makes enough
    for 4 baked pizzas)
6 ounces wild mushrooms
1 tablespoon extra virgin
    olive oil
pinch of sea salt
1½ tablespoons butter

1 tablespoon tomato sauce
    (see page 20)
2 ounces cooked ham,
    cut into small but not
    paper-thin slices
2 ounces *mozzarella fior di
    latte*, torn into 5 chunks
4 basil leaves

Place a rack on the highest shelf of the oven and turn the broiler to its highest setting. When hot, place a greased 10-inch cast-iron pan on the stove, set to medium heat.

Make the crema di ricotta: In a bowl, stir the milk into the ricotta and mix to a smooth consistency. Season with salt and pepper to taste.

Prepare the mushrooms: Rub the wild mushrooms lightly with a towel to clean. Do not wash or soak in water. Place in a bowl and toss with the olive oil and salt before cooking in the butter.

Sprinkle a little flour over your hands and on the work surface and open the dough ball by flattening and stretching the dough with your fingers, or by rolling the dough with a rolling pin. Pick the pizza base up and gently stretch it a little more over your fists without tearing it. Drop this onto the hot pan, and allow it to start rising.

As soon as the dough firms up, spread the tomato sauce over the base with the back of a metal spoon and, with a teaspoon, add blobs of *crema di ricotta* (do not spread). Scatter with the ham, basil, mushrooms, and mozzarella, and drizzle with a little extra olive oil.

Cook the pizza on top of the stove for about 3 minutes, then transfer the pan to the broiler for another 3 to 4 minutes.

Serve whole or sliced.

INGREDIENT NOTE:

For this recipe, you should use ham that is mild-flavored and possibly lightly smoked. See the method on page 57 for brining your own ham.

If you do not make your own sausage (see page 56) and have no time to prepare ground lamb (see pages 37 or 60) or Italian meatballs (see page 46), choose the chunkiest sausage you can find. To prepare the sausage, we recommend removing the skin once cooked as it enables you to distribute the meat evenly. Combining humble mushrooms and the hard bite of a little very mature cheese, this pizza has exceptional flavor.

SAUSAGE WITH FIELD MUSHROOMS & PECORINO BAKED OR SHEET

ingredients, per pizza

1 dough ball (see page 16),
   left to rise for
   1¹/₂ to 2 hours OR
   dough 2 for sheet pizzas
flour, for dusting

1¹/₂ ounces small white or
   portobello mushrooms
3 tablespoons extra virgin
   olive oil
pinch of sea salt
1 sausage
4 tablespoons tomato
   sauce (see page 20)
4 basil leaves, shredded
2 ounces *mozzarella fior di
   latte*, torn into 5 chunks
1 heaping tablespoon
   grated Pecorino

Place a rack on the highest shelf of the oven and turn the broiler to its highest setting. When hot, place a greased 10-inch cast-iron pan on the stove, set to medium heat.

Prepare the mushrooms: Clean the mushrooms by rubbing lightly with a towel. Do not wash or soak in water. Place in a bowl and toss with 1 tablespoon of the olive oil and a little salt. These mushrooms do not need to be precooked.

Prepare the sausage: Heat 1 tablespoon of the oil with a little water in a heavy pan. As the water reaches a boil, add the sausage and cook, covered, for 15 minutes, then remove the lid to allow the water to evaporate. Wait for the sausage to cool, then remove the skin.

Sprinkle a little flour over your hands and on the work surface and open the dough ball by flattening and stretching the dough with your fingers, or by rolling the dough with a rolling pin. Pick the pizza base up and gently stretch it a little more over your fists without tearing it. Drop this onto the hot pan, and allow it to start rising.

As soon as the dough firms up, spread the tomato sauce over the base with the back of a metal spoon. Drizzle with 1 tablespoon olive oil, crumble on the meat, and add the mushrooms, basil, and mozzarella, reserving half the Pecorino.

Cook the pizza on top of the stove for about 3 minutes, then transfer the pan to the broiler for another 3 to 4 minutes.

Sprinkle over the remaining Pecorino and serve whole or in slices.

For the sheet method
Follow the recipe instructions on page 19. The whole process will take about 90 minutes. Heat the oven to 500°F and stretch the dough to the edges of the baking sheet. Be sure to spread your sauce right to the edges before adding toppings. The sheet pizza dough serves 4, so quadruple the ingredient quantities. Bake for no less than 10 minutes.

Broccoli rabe tastes like a hybrid of a herb crossed with a vegetable—a delicious peppery flavor with plenty of scent. It has an "edge" that is compelling, as do olives, as does smoked cheese. Say no more.

BROCCOLI RABE, OLIVE, & SMOKED MOZZARELLA BAKED

ingredients, per pizza

1 dough ball (see page 16), left to rise for 1½ to 2 hours
flour, for dusting

for the broccoli rabe (makes enough for 4 baked pizzas)
1 tablespoon extra virgin olive oil
1 garlic clove, crushed
½ red chile, finely chopped
7 ounces broccoli rabe
sea salt

1 tablespoon tomato sauce (see page 20)
4 Kalamata olives
4 basil leaves, torn
2 ounces *mozzarella fior di latte*, torn into 5 chunks
1 ounce smoked mozzarella, torn into 4 chunks
olive oil, for drizzling

Prepare the broccoli rabe: Heat the oil in a heavy sauté pan and cook the garlic and chile over medium heat. Add the leaves, some salt, and a splash of water and cover. Cook for about 4 minutes. Drain well and squeeze excess water from the leaves before using.

Place a rack on the highest shelf of the oven and turn the broiler to its highest setting. When hot, place a greased 10-inch cast-iron pan on the stove, set to medium heat.

Sprinkle a little flour over your hands and on the work surface and open the dough ball by flattening and stretching the dough with your fingers, or by rolling the dough with a rolling pin. Pick the pizza base up and gently stretch it a little more over your fists without tearing it. Drop this onto the hot pan, and allow it to start rising.

As soon as the dough firms up, spread the tomato sauce over the base with the back of a metal spoon. Lay some broccoli rabe leaves down on the pizza and then top with the olives, basil, and both cheeses.

Cook the pizza on top of the stove for about 3 minutes, then transfer the pan to the broiler for another 3 to 4 minutes.

Once ready, drizzle with a little olive oil to finish.

INGREDIENT NOTE.

Smoked mozzarella adds a wonderful dimension to certain pizzas and can also be used in salads. If you wish to smoke your own cheese, follow the recipe on page 23.

This is a family pizza with much rolling of meatballs required, which means kids, if you have them, can get involved. Make the balls small and plentiful—the more the merrier, in every respect!

ITALIAN MEATBALLS BAKED OR SHEET

ingredients, per pizza

1 dough ball (see page 16),
    left to rise for
    1½ to 2 hours OR
    dough 2 for sheet pizzas
flour, for dusting

for the Italian meatballs
    (makes enough
    for 4 baked pizzas)
1 slice bread (no crust)
1 egg yolk
1 cup reduced tomato
    sauce (see page 20)
1 garlic clove, crushed
¼ pound ground veal
¼ pound ground beef
2 ounces mortadella
⅓ cup grated Parmesan
sea salt and freshly ground
    black pepper
1 tablespoon chopped
    flat-leaf parsley

3 ounces *mozzarella fior di
    latte*, torn into 6 chunks
4 basil leaves, torn
several shavings Parmesan
1 teaspoon chopped
    parsley
chile oil, optional
    (see page 80)

Make the meatballs: Soak the bread in the egg yolk and mash it with a fork. In a large bowl, mix all the meatball ingredients together and roll into small balls.

In a large pan, heat the tomato sauce and, when simmering, drop the meatballs in and cook for about 8 minutes.

Place a rack on the highest shelf of the oven and turn the broiler to its highest setting. When hot, place a greased 10-inch cast-iron pan on the stove, set to medium heat.

Sprinkle a little flour over your hands and on the work surface and open the dough ball by flattening and stretching the dough with your fingers, or by rolling the dough with a rolling pin. Pick the pizza base up and gently stretch it a little more over your fists without tearing it. Drop this onto the hot pan, and allow it to start rising.

As soon as the dough firms up, spread 5 meatballs with their sauce around the pizza and add the mozzarella and basil.

Cook the pizza on top of the stove for about 3 minutes, then transfer the pan to the broiler for another 3 to 4 minutes.

Once ready, finish off with the Parmesan shavings and freshly chopped parsley. Serve with chile oil on the side.

For the sheet method
Follow the recipe instructions on page 19. The whole process will take about 90 minutes. Heat the oven to 500°F and stretch the dough to the edges of the baking sheet. Be sure to spread your sauce right to the edges before adding toppings. The sheet pizza dough serves 4, so quadruple the ingredient quantities. Bake for no less than 10 minutes.

INGREDIENT NOTES

Classic Italian meatballs contain a mixture of veal, pork, and beef. Chuck is a good cut of beef for grinding.
    If you cannot find mortadella, use half ground shoulder of pork and half bacon.

MIXED LEAF SALAD

FOGLIA DI
INSALATA MISTA

This is Franco Manca's house salad recipe. Alfalfa sprouts have a lovely peppery quality, and if you have fresh, ripe avocado or fennel, both make great additional ingredients.

SERVES 4

32 cherry tomatoes, quartered
1 cup sliced and quartered cucumber
1¼ cups (1½ ounces) alfalfa sprouts
1⅓ pounds mixed leaves
a good sprig of mint leaves

MUSTARD AND HONEY VINAIGRETTE (MAKES 2 CUPS)
½ cup cider vinegar
1 teaspoon yellow mustard seeds
1 teaspoon black mustard seeds
2 teaspoons organic mustard
2 teaspoons honey
1 teaspoon dried oregano
¾ cup canola oil
½ cup extra virgin olive oil
sea salt and freshly ground black pepper, to taste

Simply wash, prep, and toss together the salad ingredients.

To make the vinaigrette: Use a blender, food processor, a small whisk, or a handheld stick blender to combine all the ingredients. Whatever you do, always start with the vinegar and other ingredients and add the oil in stages. This will make a more successful emulsion. The mustard (a protein) in the recipe helps to stabilize the emulsion so that it does not easily separate.

ARUGULA & PARMESAN SALAD

RUCOLA E
PARMIGIANO
INSALATA

A simple watercress or arugula salad works well with pizzas, dressed with shavings of Parmesan and a little balsamic vinegar.

SERVES 4

1½ pounds arugula
11 ounces Parmesan, shaved into curls
1 tablespoon balsamic vinegar
2 tablespoons extra virgin olive oil
sea salt and freshly ground black pepper

Combine all the ingredients in a large bowl and toss to mix. Season to taste.

This is a fairly hot, spicy pizza, though the heat is nicely balanced by the salty bacon. Sweet chiles are not actually that sweet, just more so than red chiles. Try to find the best-quality bacon you can find and make sure it is sliced thinly.

BACON, SWEET GREEN CHILE, & ARUGULA BAKED

ingredients, per pizza

1 dough ball (see page 16), left to rise for 1½ to 2 hours

flour, for dusting

1 sweet green chile

1 tablespoon tomato sauce (see page 20)

2 teaspoons extra virgin olive oil

3 slices bacon

4 basil leaves, torn

2 ounces *mozzarella fior di latte*, torn into 5 chunks

a handful of arugula (optional)

Place a rack on the highest shelf of the oven and turn the broiler to its highest setting. When hot, place a greased 10-inch cast-iron pan on the stove, set to medium heat.

Prepare the chile: Heat the chile over a gas burner on the naked flame, or on a hot barbecue, so that the skin burns. Keep turning until the chile is scorched and the skin starts to blister. Set aside to cool, then slice in half and scrape out the seeds.

Sprinkle a little flour over your hands and on the work surface and open the dough ball by flattening and stretching the dough with your fingers, or by rolling the dough with a rolling pin. Pick the pizza base up and gently stretch it a little more over your fists without tearing it. Drop this onto the hot pan, and allow it to start rising.

As soon as the dough firms up, spread the tomato sauce over the base using the back of a metal spoon. Drizzle with olive oil, then arrange the bacon, chile, basil, and mozzarella on top.

Cook the pizza on top of the stove for about 3 minutes, then transfer the pan to the broiler for another 3 to 4 minutes.

Once ready, dress with arugula, if you like, and serve whole or in slices.

INGREDIENT NOTE

Although the saltiness of the bacon provides balance in this recipe, it can sometimes overpower. To temper it a little, poach it in simmering water for 5 minutes before using.

The best peppers usually arrive in July and end in September. Yellow peppers are the sweetest, and you can make this pizza with yellow peppers only, if you wish. There is no mozzarella on this pizza as the freshness of the peppers is compromised by cooked cheese. Do not be tempted to adjust this—when you try it, you'll taste why.

SCORCHED RED & YELLOW
PEPPERS BAKED

ingredients, per pizza

1 dough ball (see page 16),
    left to rise for
    1½ to 2 hours
flour, for dusting

for the salsa

2 medium fresh tomatoes
½ teaspoon salt
½ garlic clove, minced
½ tablespoon finely
    chopped onion
2 basil leaves, chopped

for the peppers
    (makes enough
    for 4 baked pizzas)

2 yellow peppers
1 red pepper
½ garlic clove, minced
flat-leaf parsley, chopped,
    to taste
2 tablespoons olive oil
sea salt and freshly ground
    black pepper

Prepare the salsa: Place the tomatoes in a bowl and cover with boiling water. Leave for about 3 minutes, then remove and allow to cool slightly. Peel, seed, and chop the tomatoes. Transfer to a sieve, sprinkle with salt, and let the tomatoes drain for about 20 minutes. In a bowl, mix the tomatoes with the garlic, onion, and basil.

Prepare the peppers: Heat each pepper over a gas burner on the naked flame, or on a hot barbecue, so that the skin burns. Keep turning until the skin is black. Set aside to cool before scraping the skin away with the back of a small knife. Cut the peppers open, spoon out the seeds and cut the peppers into long strips. Transfer to a small bowl and combine with the garlic, parsley, olive oil, and a grind of pepper and a pinch of salt. Leave to marinate for 1 hour.

Place a rack on the highest shelf of the oven and turn the broiler to its highest setting. When hot, place a greased 10-inch cast-iron pan on the stove, set to medium heat.

Sprinkle a little flour over your hands and on the work surface and open the dough ball by flattening and stretching the dough with your fingers, or by rolling the dough with a rolling pin. Pick the pizza base up and gently stretch it a little more over your fists without tearing it. Drop this onto the hot pan, and allow it to start rising.

As soon as the dough firms up, turn the heat down to medium and spread the tomato salsa over the base with the back of a metal spoon. Drizzle with a little extra oil.

Cook the pizza on top of the stove for about 3 minutes, then transfer the pan to the broiler for another 3 to 4 minutes.

Once ready, add the peppers and serve in one piece or sliced.

The *Treviggiana* is a sort of radicchio that, in its *tardivo* form, looks a little like a tentacled octopus. It has more latent sweetness than other varieties, which comes through as it roasts off and caramelizes. In Treviso, a region north of Venice, where this radicchio is grown, we have even been served radicchio ice cream! It is seasonal but sometimes available through food importers.

RADICCHIO, REGGIANO, & BLUE CHEESE BAKED

ingredients, per pizza

1 dough ball (see page 16),
   left to rise for
   1½ to 2 hours
flour, for dusting

for the radicchio
   (makes enough
   for 4 baked pizzas)
¼ pound (16 leaves)
   radicchio leaves, washed
2 tablespoons olive oil
generous pinch of salt

2 teaspoons extra virgin
   olive oil
2 ounces *mozzarella fior di
   latte*, torn into 5 chunks
2 ounces blue cheese,
   crumbled into 5 chunks
4 teaspoons grated
   Parmesan
garlic oil (optional)

Prepare the radicchio: In a large bowl, mix the radicchio with the olive oil and salt and leave to marinate for 40 minutes.

Place a rack on the highest shelf of the oven and turn the broiler to its highest setting. When hot, place a greased 10-inch cast-iron pan on the stove, set to medium heat.

Sprinkle a little flour over your hands and on the work surface and open the dough ball by flattening and stretching the dough with your fingers, or by rolling the dough with a rolling pin. Pick the pizza base up and gently stretch it a little more over your fists without tearing it. Drop this onto the hot pan, and allow it to start rising.

As soon as the dough firms up, drizzle with the olive oil and add the mozzarella and marinated radicchio leaves. Top with the blue cheese and half the grated Parmesan.

Cook the pizza on top of the stove for about 3 minutes, then transfer the pan to the grill for another 3 to 4 minutes.

Dress with the remaining Parmesan and serve in pieces or whole, with an extra drizzle of garlic oil if you have it.

In Naples and the surrounding area, this combination of a juicy, thick-cut pork sausage and broccoli rabe is an autumn-winter classic. Both are favored farm ingredients and at their very best at this time of year. However, when broccoli rabe is a little hard to find, *cime di rape* (turnip tops) are often substituted and make a very good alternative.

SAUSAGE WITH BROCCOLI RABE BAKED

ingredients, per pizza

1 dough ball (see page 16),
    left to rise for
    1½ to 2 hours
flour, for dusting

**for the broccoli rabe
    (makes enough
    for 4 baked pizzas)**
2 teaspoons extra virgin
    olive oil
1 garlic clove, crushed
½ red chile, finely
    chopped
7 ounces broccoli rabe

1 sausage (see page 56)
3 ounces *mozzarella fior di
    latte*, torn into
    6 to 8 chunks
1½ tablespoons extra
    virgin olive oil
5 slices Gruyère
4 slices sweet pancetta
5 teaspoons grated
    Pecorino
2 teaspoons truffle oil
    (optional)

Prepare the broccoli rabe: Heat the oil in a heavy sauté pan and cook the garlic and chile over medium heat. Add the broccoli rabe, some salt, and a drop of water and cover. Cook for about 4 minutes. Drain well and squeeze excess water from the leaves before using.

Prepare the sausage: Set a heavy sauté pan, with enough water to coat the bottom and 1 tablespoon olive oil on the stove over medium heat. As the water comes to a boil, add the sausage and cook, covered, for about 15 minutes, then take the lid off to allow the water to evaporate. Let the sausage cool, then remove the skin.

Place a rack on the highest shelf of the oven and turn the broiler to its highest setting. When hot, place a greased 10-inch cast-iron pan on the stove, set to medium heat.

Sprinkle a little flour over your hands and on the work surface and open the dough ball by flattening and stretching the dough with your fingers, or by rolling the dough with a rolling pin. Pick the pizza base up and gently stretch it a little more over your fists without tearing it. Drop this onto the hot pan, and allow it to start rising.

As soon as the dough firms up, distribute the *broccoli rabe* over the base and add the mozzarella, Gruyère, pancetta, and a drizzle of olive oil.

Cook the pizza on top of the stove for about 3 minutes, then transfer the pan to the broiler for another 3 to 4 minutes.

Once ready, sprinkle the Pecorino over the pizza, drizzle with the truffle oil, if using, and serve whole or in slices.

MAKING YOUR OWN SAUSAGE

Making your own sausages is not difficult at all and can be a lot of fun. If you have a sausage-making machine, by all means use that, but it's not necessary at all—you just need good meat, simple flavorings, some natural sausage casing (which you can source online), and the aid of a wooden spoon or ladle handle.

Natural casings are stored in salt so should be washed before use to soften them up. Soak them in water, mixed with a little vinegar, for 1 hour (or overnight).

This sausage recipe can also be used as a delicious ground meat topping. If you would like to make it extra spicy, add 2 tablespoons chile paste (see page 80) into the mix.

MAKES APPROX 10 SAUSAGES
approx. 2 yards natural casing, washed and soaked
2 pounds pork (equal parts belly, shoulder, and neck), cold out of the fridge
1 tablespoon salt
1 teaspoon freshly ground black pepper
2 tablespoons fennel seeds
¼ cup white wine or cider

With a very sharp knife, cut the pork into small pieces. Using a knife is best but, if you have a meat grinder, you can also use this on its coarsest setting.

In a large stainless-steel, plastic, or glass bowl, mix all the ingredients together until thoroughly combined and rest in a sealed container in the fridge for 3 days, for the flavors to meld.

With the help of a funnel and the aid of a wooden spoon or ladle handle, gently stuff the sausage meat into the casing, being very careful that the skin does not tear.

After you have filled the casing, twist the sausages a few times at the lengths you desire.

Hang in a cold place (50°F) like a garland, so the sausages are kept apart and air can circulate around them. Leave them for a day, to give them extra flavor.

Hygiene note
Keep your hands, work surface, and equipment (especially knives) all super clean, and work with cold meat fresh from the fridge.

BRINING YOUR OWN HAM

As well as providing a great pizza topping, this ham will serve multiple purposes—delicious in sandwiches, salads, you name it. This recipe contains no extra spices or flavors and it rests on using a really good-quality, free-range farm animal. The best kind is from a free-range pig on a diet of just chestnuts and acorns, and this is why the best pork comes at the end of autumn or the beginning of winter. The fat they have accumulated to get them through the cold months has an incredible taste and is almost the best part of the animal.

A shoulder of ham is often very large, so you can also use a shoulder of pork, which is similar and also very tasty. Make sure that the shoulder bone (scapula) is removed, or it will inhibit the brining.

boned shoulder of ham
¼ cup salt
1 teaspoon sugar per quart of water

Place the ham in a large saucepan, cover with water, and bring to the boil. Add the salt and a teaspoon of sugar per quart of water, then take off the heat and allow to cool. Cover the container and set aside in the fridge or a cold garage for 8 days.

Discard the brine and rinse the ham quickly under cold running water. Clean out the container, then place the brined shoulder back in the pot and cover with water. Place on the heat and bring to a simmer, add the salt and sugar again as before, and leave to cook for 10 to 12 minutes per pound of meat. Try to keep the water at a brisk simmer if you can.

Remove the ham from the brine and pat dry with paper towels, then place on a wire rack to cool completely.

If you would like a caramelized finish, roast the ham briefly with a glaze of molasses, or simply store as it is.

You can use homemade sausage in the following recipes:

Sausage with Mushrooms & Pecorino p. 43
Sausage with Broccoli Rabe p. 55
Pork Sausage with Roasted Peppers & Parmesan p. 58

You can use home-brined ham in the following recipe:

Ham, Mushrooms, & Ricotta p. 42

The mix of garlic, capers, basil, and roasted peppers in this recipe acts like a single ingredient to balance the meatiness of the sausage. Pork sausage works best, as it is lighter in flavor than beef, although lamb can also be used.

PORK SAUSAGE, ROASTED PEPPERS, & PARMESAN   BAKED OR SHEET

ingredients, per pizza

1 dough ball (see page 16),
   left to rise for
   1½ to 2 hours OR
   dough 2 for sheet pizzas
flour, for dusting

for the peppers with capers and garlic (makes enough for 4 pizzas)
2 garlic cloves, crushed
½ teaspoon salt
5 basil leaves, torn
4 capers
7 ounces roasted red
   peppers, cut into long
   strips (see page 52)

1 sausage (see page 56)
2 teaspoons olive oil
4 teaspoons grated
   Parmesan
4 basil leaves, torn
a handful of arugula
   (optional)

Make the roasted peppers: In a large bowl, mix all the ingredients together and leave to marinate for 1 hour before using.

Prepare the sausage: Set a heavy sauté pan, with enough water to coat the bottom and 1 tablespoon olive oil on the stove over medium heat. As the water comes to the boil, add the sausage and cook, covered, for about 15 minutes, then take the lid off and allow the water to evaporate. Let the sausage cool, then remove the skin.

Place a rack on the highest shelf of the oven and turn the broiler to its highest setting. When hot, place a greased 10-inch cast-iron pan on the stove, set to medium heat.

Sprinkle a little flour over your hands and on the work surface and open the dough ball by flattening and stretching the dough with your fingers, or by rolling the dough with a rolling pin. Pick the pizza base up and gently stretch it a little more over your fists without tearing it. Drop this onto the hot pan, and allow it to start rising.

As soon as the dough firms up, turn the heat down to medium and drizzle the base with olive oil. Add a quarter of the roasted pepper mix, the Parmesan, basil, and cooked sausage.

Cook the pizza on top of the stove for about 3 minutes, then transfer the pan to the broiler for another 3 to 4 minutes.

Once this is ready, scatter with arugula, if using, and serve in one piece or sliced.

For the sheet method
Follow the recipe instructions on page 19. The whole process will take about 90 minutes. Heat the oven to 500°F and stretch the dough to the edges of the baking sheet. Be sure to spread your sauce right to the edges before adding toppings. The sheet pizza dough serves 4, so quadruple the ingredient quantities. Bake for no less than 10 minutes.

If you want to get hot without getting too heavy, this is the pizza for you. Make your lamb mix as spicy as you dare and balance with tangy tomato sauce (reduced if you prefer a punchier flavor) and your molten mozzarella.

SPICY LAMB, MOZZARELLA, & TOMATO BAKED OR SHEET

ingredients, per pizza

1 dough ball (see page 16),
   left to rise for
   1 1/2 to 2 hours OR
   dough 2 for sheet pizzas
flour, for dusting

for the spicy lamb
   (makes enough
   for 4 baked pizzas)
1 tablespoon olive oil
4 garlic cloves, 3 roasted,
   1 finely chopped
2/3 scotch bonnet chile,
   seeded and chopped
a pinch of paprika
10 ounces lamb (or ground
   lamb)

2 teaspoons extra virgin
   olive oil
1 tablespoon tomato sauce
   (see page 20)
4 basil leaves, torn
2 ounces *mozzarella fior di
   latte*, torn into 6 chunks
4 teaspoons grated
   Pecorino
1 teaspoon garlic oil
   (optional)

Make the spicy lamb: Heat the oil in a heavy sauté pan and cook the garlic and chile slowly over low heat until the garlic browns. Remove from the heat and add the paprika. Remove the skin from the roasted garlic, then place everything in a large bowl with the meat and grind together. (If using already ground meat, combine thoroughly.) Leave to marinate before using.

Place a rack on the highest shelf of the oven and turn the broiler to its highest setting. When hot, place a greased 10-inch cast-iron pan on the stove, set to medium heat.

Sprinkle a little flour over your hands and on the work surface, and open the dough ball by flattening and stretching the dough with your fingers, or by rolling the dough with a rolling pin. Pick the pizza base up and gently stretch it a little more over your fists without tearing it. Drop this onto the hot pan, and allow it to start rising.

As soon as the dough firms up, spread the tomato sauce over the base with the back of a spoon. Distribute a quarter of the lamb over the top and add the rest of the ingredients, reserving some Pecorino to finish.

Cook the pizza on top of the stove for about 3 minutes, then transfer the pan to the broiler for another 3 to 4 minutes.

Once ready, sprinkle with the remaining Pecorino, drizzle with garlic oil, if using, and serve in one piece or sliced.

For the sheet method
Follow the recipe instructions on page 19. The whole process will take about 90 minutes. Heat the oven to 500°F and stretch the dough to the edges of the baking sheet. Be sure to spread your sauce right to the edges before adding toppings. The sheet pizza dough serves 4, so quadruple the ingredient quantities. Bake for no less than 10 minutes.

Caramelized onion with pancetta or bacon is a great pairing but we also love the vegetarian combination of blue cheese and spinach. For blue cheese, we use Stilton, along with a fairly firm goat cheese. The spinach is simply seared with a little garlic oil.

SPINACH, CARAMELIZED ONION, GOAT CHEESE, & BLUE CHEESE BAKED

ingredients, per pizza

1 dough ball (see page 16), left to rise for 1½ to 2 hours
flour, for dusting

for the caramelized onion (makes enough for 4 baked pizzas)

1 large onion, thinly sliced in rings
2 teaspoons olive oil
1 teaspoon sugar
½ teaspoon vinegar

for the spinach (makes enough for 4 baked pizzas)

2 teaspoons extra virgin olive oil
½ red chile, finely chopped (optional)
1 garlic clove, crushed
9 ounces spinach
pinch of sea salt

2 teaspoons olive oil
1 ounce blue cheese
1 ounce goat cheese
2 ounces *mozzarella fior di latte*, torn into 5 chunks

Make the caramelized onion: Heat the oil in a frying pan and sweat the onion over low heat for about 20 minutes. Add a bit of water if it starts to stick. (If the onion burns, discard it.) When it has turned a golden color, stir in the sugar and vinegar and reduce the temperature even more. After about 15 minutes, the onion should have caramelized.

Prepare the spinach: Heat the oil in a heavy sauté pan and cook the chile and garlic. Add the spinach, salt, and a drop of water and cover. Cook for about 4 minutes. Drain well and squeeze out excess water before using.

Place a rack on the highest shelf of the oven and turn the broiler to its highest setting. When hot, place a greased 10-inch cast-iron pan on the stove, set to medium heat.

Sprinkle a little flour over your hands and on the work surface and open the dough ball by flattening and stretching the dough with your fingers, or by rolling the dough with a rolling pin. Pick the pizza base up and gently stretch it a little more over your fists without tearing it. Drop this onto the hot pan, and allow it to start rising.

As soon as the dough firms up, drizzle with the olive oil and distribute a quarter of the caramelized onion and spinach over the base, and top with the blue cheese, goat cheese, and mozzarella.

Cook the pizza on top of the stove for about 3 minutes, then transfer the pan to the broiler for another 3 to 4 minutes.

Serve whole or in slices.

Butternut squash is a wonderful ingredient that we prefer to
the usual pumpkins available in Italy. It caramelizes beautifully
in the oven, and its sweetness, offset by the blue cheese,
makes this pizza work very well. The roasted pine nuts are
simply a decadent addition.

BLUE CHEESE, BUTTERNUT SQUASH,
& PINE NUTS BAKED

ingredients, per pizza

1 dough ball (see page 16),
  left to rise for
  1½ to 2 hours
flour, for dusting

for the butternut squash
(makes enough
for 4 baked pizzas)

6 ounces butternut
  squash, peeled and cut
  into small wedges
2 tablespoons extra virgin
  olive oil
sea salt

2 teaspoons pine nuts
2 teaspoons extra virgin
  olive oil
2 ounces *mozzarella fior di
  latte*, torn into 6 chunks
1 ounce blue cheese,
  crumbled into 5 chunks
3 teaspoons basil pesto
  (see page 34)

Prepare the butternut squash: Preheat the oven to 425°F. Coat the wedges
in olive oil, sprinkle with salt and bake in the oven for 40 minutes,
turning once. Reduce the heat to 350°F after 20 minutes.

Scatter the pine nuts onto a baking sheet and roast under the
broil until golden, being careful not to let them burn. Set aside.

Place a rack on the highest shelf of the oven and turn the broiler
up to its highest setting. When hot, place a greased 10-inch cast-
iron pan on the stove, set to medium heat.

Sprinkle a little flour over your hands and on the work surface
and open the dough ball by flattening and stretching the dough
with your fingers, or by rolling the dough with a rolling pin.
Pick the pizza base up and gently stretch it a little more over your
fists without tearing it. Drop this onto the hot pan, and allow it to
start rising.

As soon as the dough firms up, drizzle with olive oil and distribute
the butternut squash over the base. Scatter on the mozzarella and
blue cheese.

Cook the pizza on top of the stove for about 3 minutes, then
transfer the pan to the broiler for another 3 to 4 minutes.

Before serving, use a teaspoon to dot the pizza with basil pesto and
sprinkle with the toasted pine nuts.

The small, fruity tomatoes cut through the richness of the salami and smoked mozzarella on this pizza, particularly if you roast the cherry tomatoes to enhance their sweetness. Otherwise, the tomatoes can be baked or added fresh at the end.

SALAMI, SMOKED BUFFALO CHEESE, & CHERRY TOMATOES BAKED

ingredients, per pizza

1 dough ball (see page 16),
   left to rise for
   1 1/2 to 2 hours
flour, for dusting

2 teaspoons extra virgin
   olive oil
8 slices salami ('nduja,
   if possible)
5 cherry tomatoes, halved
2 ounces smoked buffalo
   mozzarella, torn into
   5 chunks
a handful of arugula
a few grinds of black
   pepper

Place a rack on the highest shelf of the oven and turn the broiler to its highest setting. When hot, place a greased 10-inch cast-iron pan on the stove, set to medium heat.

Sprinkle a little flour over your hands and on the work surface and open the dough ball by flattening and stretching the dough with your fingers, or by rolling the dough with a rolling pin. Pick the pizza base up and gently stretch it a little more over your fists without tearing it. Drop this onto the hot pan, and allow it to start rising.

As soon as the dough firms up, drizzle the olive oil over the base. Lay the salami on the pizza, then add the cherry tomatoes and mozzarella.

Cook the pizza on top of the stove for about 3 minutes, then transfer the pan to the broiler for another 3 to 4 minutes.

Once ready, dress with arugula and serve with a grind of black pepper and a little more olive oil.

INGREDIENT NOTE

Use 'nduja if you can, a wonderful spicy Calabrian salami that is so soft it is almost spreadable. The fat melts into the pizza and moistens the base. See the method for making your own on page 69.

Guanciale, or cured pig cheek, is sweeter than pancetta and smells even better than bacon. It is very fatty and rich and, all in all, heavenly (find the method on page 70 for how to make your own). Since melted cheese has a fairly oily texture, you are better off using fresh buffalo cheese in this recipe. The potato, though quite "dry," doesn't actually absorb excess fat, but certainly benefits from its presence in terms of flavor.

SMOKED MOZZARELLA, BAKED POTATO, & GUANCIALE BAKED OR SHEET

BAKED or Sheet

ingredients, per pizza

1 dough ball (see page 16), left to rise for 1½ to 2 hours OR dough 2 for sheet pizzas
flour, for dusting

for the potato topping (makes enough for 4 baked pizzas)

11 ounces potatoes, cut into small wedges
3 tablespoons olive oil
1 teaspoon fine sea salt
½ onion, finely sliced
½ cup halved cherry tomatoes

2 teaspoons extra virgin olive oil
1½ ounces guanciale, thinly sliced
2 ounces smoked mozzarella, torn into 5 chunks
1 ounce buffalo mozzarella, torn into 4 chunks
1 heaping tablespoon grated Parmesan

Make the potato topping: Preheat the oven to 400°F. In a roasting pan, mix the potatoes with 2 tablespoons olive oil and sea salt, and bake in the oven for about 40 minutes. Drain on paper towels.

Heat 1 tablespoon olive oil in a heavy sauté pan over low heat and sweat the onion. Turn up the heat slightly and add the cherry tomatoes. When the ingredients caramelize and become sticky, add the potato wedges and turn off the heat.

Place a rack on the highest shelf of the oven and turn the broiler to its highest setting. When hot, place a greased 10-inch cast-iron pan on the stove, set to medium heat.

Sprinkle a little flour over your hands and on the work surface and open the dough ball by flattening and stretching the dough with your fingers, or by rolling the dough with a rolling pin. Pick the pizza base up and gently stretch it a little more over your fists without tearing it. Drop this onto the hot pan, and allow it to start rising.

As soon as the dough firms up, turn the heat down to medium and drizzle the olive oil over the base. Arrange the guanciale, mozzarella and a quarter of the potatoes on top and sprinkle with half the Parmesan.

Cook the pizza on top of the stove for about 3 minutes, then transfer the pan to the broiler for another 3 to 4 minutes.

Once ready, finish with a few clumps of fresh buffalo mozzarella and sprinkle with the remaining Parmesan.

For the sheet method

Follow the recipe instructions on page 19. The whole process will take about 90 minutes. Heat the oven to 500°F and stretch the dough to the edges of the baking sheet. Be sure to spread your sauce right to the edges before adding toppings. The sheet pizza dough serves 4, so quadruple the ingredient quantities. Bake for no less than 10 minutes.

CURING

It is well worth curing at home, as all you need is good-quality meat, curing salts, and the right ambient environment—either a cellar with a temperature of 50 to 54°F and a good level of humidity (about 85%), or a fermentation cell. Unless you have the latter, curing should take place during the cooler months of the year.

Curing salts
The dry climate of southern Italy creates the perfect curing environment, where bad bacteria rarely thrive, so our recipes simply use coarse sea salt rather than curing salts. However, sadly, it is difficult to recreate such a climate at home and, to be on the safe side, it is advisable to use curing salts, which will protect against botulism.

SALAMI

SALSICCIA SECCA

This basic salami cures in just 2 weeks. It has no time to develop the classic exterior mold but it is very tasty and easy to make.

MAKES ABOUT 3 TO 4 THIN SALAMI
2 pounds pork (equal parts belly, shoulder, and neck),
  cold out of the fridge
1½ tablespoons salt (or curing salts)
½ tablespoon vinegar
1 heaping tablespoon freshly ground black pepper
1 tablespoon fennel seeds, optional
2 feet natural sausage casing, washed and soaked
butcher's string, for tying

Variation
You can make a spicy version by adding about 1 tablespoon of the chile paste from page 80.

With a very sharp knife, cut the pork into small pieces. Using a knife is best but if you have a meat grinder you can use this on its coarsest setting.

In a large stainless-steel, plastic, or glass bowl, mix all the ingredients together until thoroughly combined. With the help of a funnel and a wooden spoon handle, gently stuff the meat into the casing, filling to approx. 10 inches and then tying off with butcher's string. Pack the meat tightly so no air gets trapped and prick the sausage all over to release any air that is left.

Hang the salami in a warm, humid environment for 12 hours. This is what we call *stufatura*, which starts the fermentation process. One way to do this is to hang the salami over a pan of simmering water on the stove, or to place a large bowl of hot water under the hanging meat (refresh the hot water 3 to 4 times over 12 hours).

Transfer the salami to a cellar or fermentation cell with a temperature of 50 to 54°F and a humidity level of about 85%. After 2 weeks your salami will be ready.

SPICY CALABRIAN SALAMI

'NDUJA

This is a very soft, fatty, almost spreadable salami that works wonders on pizza. The spiciness will depend on the strength of the chile. You might use anything from hot scotch bonnets to very mild ancho chiles. The latter can be slightly roasted before use, which will add good extra flavor.

MAKES ABOUT 3 TO 4 THIN SALAMI

$2^1/_4$ pounds pork (approx. 14 ounces shoulder, 1 pound cheek, and 3 ounces back fat)
1 tablespoon salt (or curing salts)
3 ounces dried red pepper flakes
$1^1/_2$ tablespoons chili powder (or pimienton or Hungarian paprika)
1 yard natural sausage casing, washed and soaked
butcher's string, for tying

In a meat grinder, chop the meat to a very fine grind. If you do not have one, use a sharp butcher's knife and work until you have a very fine grain.

In a large stainless-steel, plastic, or glass bowl, mix all the ingredients together until thoroughly combined. With the help of a funnel and a wooden spoon handle, gently stuff the meat into the casing, filling to approx. 10 inches and then tying off with butcher's string. Pack the meat tightly so no air gets trapped and prick the sausage all over to release any air that is left.

Hang the 'nduja in a warm, humid environment for 12 hours. One way to do this is to hang the salami over a pan of simmering water on the stove or to place a large bowl of hot water under the hanging meat. Refresh the hot water 3 to 4 times over 12 hours.

Transfer the 'nduja to a cellar or fermentation cell with a temperature of 50 to 54°F and a humidity level of about 85%. After 3 to 4 weeks it will be ready.

Preserving salami
One very effective way of preserving salami is to cut it into small pieces and pack into a sterilized, sealable jar. Pack in as much salami as possible. Gently melt some lard (or other animal fat), without allowing it to cook, and pour into the jar until it reaches the top. Seal and store in a cool, dark place for up to 6 months. Once opened, keep sealed in the fridge and add a teaspoon to a pizza, or when making sauces, to add flavor.

GUANCIALE

PIG CHEEK

This is similar to bacon but the meat is taken from the cheek bone. It is fattier than bacon and has a sweet finish that works very well on pizza. You can substitute this for bacon in any of the recipes in this book.

pig cheek (a triangular shape with thick skin on one side)
coarse salt (to cover), or curing salt
2 tablespoons white wine
2 tablespoons vinegar
freshly ground black pepper or red pepper flakes (to cover)

Roll the meat in the coarse salt and place in a sealed container in the fridge or in a cool place (40 to 48°F). Rotate every day for 6 days.

After 6 days, mix the wine and vinegar together in a bowl. Scrub the salt off the meat and lightly wash the flesh side in the wine-vinegar mixture. Pat dry with paper towels.

Make a hole in one end of the meat and pass a kitchen rod through it for hanging. Cover the flesh and the hole in either ground black pepper or red pepper flakes, or wrap in a cloth to keep flies away.

Hang in a cellar or fermentation cell with a temperature of 50 to 54°F and a humidity level of about 85%. After 5 weeks your guanciale will be ready.

When cooking, remove the pepper coating from the meat.

BRESAOLA

ITALIAN
AIR–CURED
BEEF

The best meat to use for bresaola is that from a large steer. The cut is usually referred to as a "round roast," or *magatello* in Italian. However, you can also use a rolled haunch of venison.

You can easily source bungs (large, natural meat casings) on the internet. Like natural sausage casings, ox bungs must be washed in a water and vinegar solution before use.

Bresaola makes a very good antipasto on its own, with pepper, oil, and lemon. Slice as thinly as possible.

$^2/_3$ cup coarse sea salt
$1^1/_2$ tablespoons freshly ground black pepper
$^1/_2$ teaspoon sugar
$2^1/_4$ pounds beef top round
1 ox bung
butcher's string

In a container, mix the salt, pepper, and sugar together and roll the beef in this mixture, coating thoroughly. Refrigerate, turning and massaging the meat every day for 9 days (larger cuts will need longer).

After 9 days, push the meat into the ox bung and tie off the ends tightly with butcher's string. Hang in a warm environment (70°F) with an ideal humidity of 70% for 2 days. To ensure it is not too dry, place a bowl of hot water under the beef so the rising humidity can reach it. Repeat this once a day.

After 2 days, move the bresaola to a cellar or curing chamber with a temperature of 53 to 59°F for 28 days. Once the meat has lost one-third of its weight, it is ready to taste. Either vacuum-pack or wrap in foil, and use within a few weeks.

CURED LARD

LARDO

This is cured back fat and, if you chop it very finely, it will melt quickly on a pizza to delicious effect. Use in very small quantities.

1 to 4 pounds pork back fat
coarse sea salt (to cover)
freshly ground black pepper (to cover)

Cover the fat in coarse sea salt and place in a sealed container in the fridge or in a cool place (40 to 48°F). Rotate every day for 5 (for 1 pound) to 8 (for 4 pounds) days.

Cover the fat in pepper and hang in a cellar or fermentation cell with a temperature of 50 to 54°F and a humidity level of about 80%. After 4 weeks your lardo will be ready.

You can use any mix of wild mushrooms for this pizza, including oyster, chanterelles, porcini, etc., depending on what is available (do not be tempted to pick these in the wild unless you know what you are doing). Although not as exotic, cultivated mushrooms can also be used.

WILD MUSHROOM BAKED, SHEET, OR FRIED

ingredients, per pizza

1 dough ball (see page 16),
   left to rise for
   1½ to 2 hours OR
   dough 2 for sheet pizzas
flour, for dusting

for the wild mushrooms
   (makes enough
   for 4 baked pizzas)
6 ounces wild mushrooms
1 tablespoon butter
1 tablespoon extra virgin
   olive oil
pinch of sea salt

for the *crema di ricotta*
   (makes enough
   for 1 baked pizza)
2 teaspoons milk
1 heaping tablespoon
   ricotta
salt and freshly ground
   black pepper

2 teaspons extra virgin
   olive oil
2 ounces *mozzarella fior di
   latte*, torn into 5 chunks
garlic-infused olive oil
   (optional)

Prepare the wild mushrooms: Rub the wild mushrooms with a damp towel to remove any dirt. Do not soak them in water or they will become slimy. Heat the olive oil and butter in a frying pan over low heat and sear the wild mushrooms for about 3 minutes, seasoning with a pinch of salt. If you are using cultivated mushrooms, simply rub them clean and thinly slice (they do not need to be precooked).

Make the crema di ricotta: In a bowl, stir the milk into the ricotta and mix to a smooth consistency. Season with salt and pepper to taste.

Place a rack on the highest shelf of the oven and turn the broiler to its highest setting. When hot, place a greased 10-inch cast-iron pan on the stove, set to medium heat.

Sprinkle a little flour over your hands and on the work surface and open the dough ball by flattening and stretching the dough with your fingers, or by rolling the dough with a rolling pin. Pick the pizza base up and gently stretch it a little more over your fists without tearing it. Drop this onto the hot pan, and allow it to start rising.

As soon as the base firms up, spread the *crema di ricotta* over the base with the back of a metal spoon. Drizzle with the olive oil and scatter the mushrooms and mozzarella on top.

Cook the pizza on top of the stove for about 3 minutes, then transfer the pan to the broiler for another 3 to 4 minutes.

Serve in one piece or sliced, with a drizzle of garlic-infused olive oil, if you like.

For fried pizza, see the method on page 17

For the sheet method
Follow the recipe instructions on page 19. The whole process will take about 90 minutes. Heat the oven to 500°F and stretch the dough to the edges of the sheet. Be sure to spread your sauce right to the edges before adding toppings. The sheet pizza dough serves 4, so quadruple the ingredient quantities. Bake for no less than 10 minutes.

The radicchio is bitter, the caramelized onion is sweet, and the blue cheese is creamy and sharp, giving this pizza seriously strong and sensual flavors. It is advisable to eat this pizza when you are feeling very grown up.

RADICCHIO, CARAMELIZED ONION, MOZZARELLA, & PECORINO BAKED

ingredients, per pizza

1 dough ball (see page 16), left to rise for 1½ to 2 hours

flour, for dusting

for the radicchio (makes enough for 4 baked pizzas)

4 ounces (16 leaves) radicchio

2 tablespoons extra virgin olive oil

generous pinch of salt

for the caramelized onion (makes enough for 4 baked pizzas)

1 large onion, thinly sliced

2 teaspoons olive oil

1 teaspoon sugar

½ teaspoon vinegar

2 ounces *mozzarella fior di latte*, torn into 5 chunks

5 teaspoons grated Pecorino

1 tablespoon tomato sauce (see page 20)

2 teaspoons extra virgin olive oil

Prepare the radicchio: In a large bowl, mix the radicchio with the olive oil and salt and leave to marinate for 40 minutes.

Make the caramelized onion: Heat the olive oil in a frying pan over low heat and sweat the onion for about 20 minutes. Add a little water if it starts to stick. (If the onion burns, discard it.) When it has turned a golden color, stir in the sugar and vinegar and reduce the temperature more. After about 15 minutes, the onions should have caramelized.

Place a rack on the highest shelf of the oven and turn the broiler to its highest setting. When hot, place a greased 10-inch cast-iron pan on the stove, set to medium heat.

Sprinkle a little flour over your hands and on the work surface and open the dough ball by flattening and stretching the dough with your fingers, or by rolling the dough with a rolling pin. Pick the pizza base up and gently stretch it a little more over your fists without tearing it. Drop this onto the hot pan, and allow it to start rising.

As soon as the dough firms up, spread the tomato sauce over the base with the back of a metal spoon. Distribute a quarter of the caramelized onions on top, then a quarter of the radicchio, and then add the radicchio, mozzarella, and Pecorino.

Cook the pizza on top of the stove for about 3 minutes, then transfer the pan to the broiler for another 3 to 4 minutes.

Serve whole or in slices.

Chorizo is a wonderful Iberian pork sausage, made with smoked red peppers (pimenton), which comes in both fresh and dried varieties. Countries as diverse as Hungary and Mexico make good versions of chorizo-like pork sausage. In fact, anywhere known for its smoked paprikas and chiles (or plant varieties of the genus *Capsicum*) often has pork products that are worth a try.

CHORIZO BAKED OR SHEET

ingredients, per pizza

1 dough ball (see page 16), left to rise for 1½ to 2 hours OR dough 2 for sheet pizzas

flour, for dusting

2 teaspoons extra virgin olive oil

1 garlic clove, peeled and roughly chopped

1 tablespoon tomato sauce (see page 20)

about 7 slices chorizo

6 to 8 chunks cooking chorizo

2 ounces *mozzarella fior di latte*, torn into 5 chunks

4 basil leaves, torn

freshly ground black pepper

In a saucepan, heat the oil and cook the garlic over low heat until lightly golden. Stir in the tomato sauce.

Place a rack on the highest shelf of the oven and turn the broiler to its highest setting. When hot, place a greased 10-inch cast-iron pan on the stove, set to medium heat.

Sprinkle a little flour over your hands and on the work surface and open the dough ball by flattening and stretching the dough with your fingers, or by rolling the dough with a rolling pin. Pick the pizza base up and gently stretch it a little more over your fists without tearing it. Drop this onto the hot pan, and allow it to start rising.

As soon as the dough firms up, spread the tomato and garlic sauce over the base with the back of a metal spoon. Scatter the chorizo and mozzarella on top.

Cook the pizza on top of the stove for about 3 minutes, then transfer the pan to the broiler for another 3 to 4 minutes.

Once ready, scatter the basil leaves on top and serve with a few grinds of pepper, in one piece or sliced.

For the sheet method

Follow the recipe instructions on page 19. The whole process will take about 90 minutes. Heat the oven to 500°F and stretch the dough to the edges of the baking sheet. Be sure to spread your sauce right to the edges before adding toppings. The sheet pizza dough serves 4, so quadruple the ingredient quantities. Bake for no less than 10 minutes.

INGREDIENT NOTE

Avoid boiled and smoked sausages and the less fatty varieties, but try products such as Calabrian 'nduja. The fat runs as it cooks, becoming a tasty capsicum-infused oil, which makes a very juicy pizza.

This pizza is very satisfying. The blue cheese and pancetta work well together, and the sweet onion adds complexity. Although a little on the rich side, this pizza might well be recommended as the perfect hangover cure after a big night out.

PANCETTA, CARAMELIZED ONION, & BLUE CHEESE BAKED OR SHEET

ingredients, per pizza

1 dough ball (see page 16), left to rise for 1½ to 2 hours OR dough 2 for sheet pizzas

flour, for dusting

2 teaspoons extra virgin olive oil

2 ounces blue cheese, broken into 5 chunks

4 slices pancetta

2 ounces *mozzarella fior di latte*, torn into 5 chunks

for the caramelized onion (makes enough for 4 baked pizzas)

1 large onion, thinly sliced

2 teaspoons olive oil

1 teaspoon sugar

½ teaspoon vinegar

Make the caramelized onion: Heat the olive oil in a frying pan over low heat and sweat the onion for about 20 minutes. Add a little water if it starts to stick. (If the onion burns, discard it.) When it has turned a golden color, stir in the sugar and vinegar and reduce the temperature more. After about 15 minutes, the onion should have caramelized.

Place a rack on the highest shelf of the oven and turn the broiler to its highest setting. When hot, place a greased 10-inch cast-iron pan on the stove, set to medium heat.

Sprinkle a little flour over your hands and on the work surface and open the dough ball by flattening and stretching the dough with your fingers, or by rolling the dough with a rolling pin. Pick the pizza base up and gently stretch it a little more over your fists without tearing it. Drop this onto the hot pan, and allow it to start rising.

As soon as the dough firms up, drizzle the base with olive oil and distribute a quarter of the caramelized onion on top, then add the blue cheese, pancetta, and mozzarella.

Cook the pizza on top of the stove for about 3 minutes, then transfer the pan to the broiler for another 3 to 4 minutes.

Serve whole or in slices.

For the sheet method

Follow the recipe instructions on page 19. The whole process will take about 90 minutes. Heat the oven to 500°F and stretch the dough to the edges of the baking sheet. Be sure to spread your sauce right to the edges before adding toppings. The sheet pizza dough serves 4, so quadruple the ingredient quantities. Bake for no less than 10 minutes.

This pizza presents a subtle mix of flavors that works like a dream—the blue cheese is tangy and scented, the goat cheese is austere, while the mozzarella and washed rind cheeses add creamy bass notes. The bitter, crunchy radicchio cuts through the richness of them all, making this an almost decadent but extremely delicious pizza.

MIXED CHEESE WITH
RADICCHIO *BAKED*

ingredients, per pizza

1 dough ball (see page 16),
   left to rise for
   1½ to 2 hours
flour, for dusting

**for the radicchio
   (makes enough
   for 4 baked pizzas)**
5 ounces (16 leaves)
   radicchio
2 tablespoons extra virgin
   olive oil
generous pinch of salt

2 teaspoons extra virgin
   olive oil
½ ounce washed rind
   cheese
½ ounce goat cheese,
   crumbled
½ ounce blue cheese,
   crumbled
3 ounces *mozzarella fior di
   latte*, torn into 6 chunks
4 basil leaves, torn

Prepare the radicchio: In a large bowl, mix the radicchio with the olive oil and salt and leave to marinate for 40 minutes.

Place a rack on the highest shelf of the oven and turn the broiler to its highest setting. When hot, place a greased 10-inch cast-iron pan on the stove, set to medium heat.

Sprinkle a little flour over your hands and on the work surface and open the dough ball by flattening and stretching the dough with your fingers, or by rolling the dough with a rolling pin. Pick the pizza base up and gently stretch it a little more over your fists without tearing it. Drop this onto the hot pan, and allow it to start rising.

As soon as the dough firms up, drizzle the base with olive oil, then add all the cheeses, the basil and a quarter of the marinated radicchio leaves.

Cook the pizza on top of the stove for about 3 minutes, then transfer the pan to the broiler for another 3 to 4 minutes.

Serve whole or in slices.

INGREDIENT NOTE

In late winter/early spring you may find *Tardivo* (or to give it its full name: *Radicchio Rosso di Treviso Tardivo*), which is a very special sweet radicchio that looks a little like a tentacled octopus. If this is the case, slice it in half lengthwise, rub with olive oil, salt and freshly ground pepper, and sear it in a hot pan.

CHILE OIL

OLIO AL PEPERONCINO

1 QUART
14 ounces scotch bonnet chiles (including seeds), chopped
3 tablespoons paprika (optional)
³/₄ cup peanut oil
3¹/₂ cups olive oil

Place the chiles, peanut oil, and paprika (if using—it will add color) in a heavy sauté pan and warm over very low heat—the oil should never be above 285°F—until the chiles have lost all their water content (about 30 minutes). The smoke from this will make you choke, so open the kitchen windows beforehand!

Remove the pan from the heat and add the olive oil. Allow to cool, then transfer to a covered container for 48 hours. Filter well through a sieve and store in sterilized bottles or jars in a cool, dark place for up to a year.

CHILE PASTE

This is great for flavoring sausages or meatballs (see page 46). The best chiles to use are the red ones available toward the end of the season, when they are a little dry.

MAKES **7** OUNCES
14 ounces red chiles, cut into strips and seeds removed

Preheat the oven to 265°F. Place the chiles skin-side down in a roasting pan, cover generously with water, and bake in the oven for about 2 hours, until the water has evaporated. (Keep an eye on them to avoid browning.)

Reduce the oven temperature to 195°F and bake for another 2 hours, by which time you will be left with a paste similar in consistency to that of tomato paste.

Pass the paste through a food mill using a sieve fine enough to retain the skin and the seeds, if any remain.

Bottle the paste in a sterilized, sealable container and store in a cool, dark place for up to a year.

Variation
You can make a non-hot version using red peppers instead of chiles, or a milder version using a mixture of red peppers and chiles. You could also try mixing large green ancho chiles with red chiles for a different flavor.

Goat curd is light and has a good acidity that complements the meaty strength of the salami well. You need a soft salami, like *finocchiona* or even *ciauscolo* or *'nduja*—a spicy, spreadable sausage that you can add in small pieces. In Majorca, they make a very soft *sobrasada*, which is also very good for this pizza.

SALAMI & GOAT CURD   BAKED

ingredients, per pizza

1 dough ball (see page 16),
   left to rise for
   1¹/₂ to 2 hours
flour, for dusting

1 tablespoon tomato sauce
   (see page 20)
2 teaspoons extra virgin
   olive oil
8 slices salami
2 ounces *mozzarella fior di
   latte*, torn into 5 chunks
1 ounce goat curd, sliced
a handful of arugula or
   watercress
freshly ground black
   pepper
chile oil, optional
   (see page 80)

Place a rack on the highest shelf of the oven and turn the broiler to its highest setting. When hot, place a greased 10-inch cast-iron pan on the stove, set to medium heat.

Sprinkle a little flour over your hands and on the work surface and open the dough ball by flattening and stretching the dough with your fingers, or by rolling the dough with a rolling pin. Pick the pizza base up and gently stretch it a little more over your fists without tearing it. Drop this onto the hot pan, and allow it to start rising.

As soon as the dough firms up, spread the tomato sauce over the base using the back of a metal spoon. Drizzle with the olive oil and lay down the salami and mozzarella on top.

Cook the pizza on top of the stove for about 3 minutes, then transfer the pan to the broiler for another 3 to 4 minutes.

Once ready, spread the goat curd evenly over the pizza, dress with arugula (or watercress in summer), and serve whole, with a grind of black pepper and more olive oil or chile oil. The latter complements this recipe very well.

The flavors of this pizza are mild and sweet—perfect for a hot or breezy summer's day. The zucchini is cooked with mint, which complements its light sweetness, and the mild, cool goat curd within the fresh zucchini flowers contributes blissfully to this effect. The flowers themselves make a lovely decoration, too.

ZUCCHINI, GRUYÈRE, & GOAT CURD BAKED

ingredients, per pizza

1 dough ball (see page 16), left to rise for 1½ to 2 hours
flour, for dusting

for the zucchini (makes enough for four baked pizzas)

1 medium zucchini, thinly sliced
1 teaspoon olive oil
10 basil leaves, torn
a pinch of salt
5 mint leaves, chopped

for the zucchini flowers (makes enough for four baked pizzas)

4 zucchini flowers
4 tablespoons goat curd
salt and freshly ground black pepper

2 teaspoons extra virgin olive oil
4 basil leaves
1 ounce sliced Gruyère
2 ounces *mozzarella fior di latte*, torn into 5 chunks

Prepare the zucchini: Place the zucchini in a wide, shallow pan, and stir in the oil and basil. Place, covered, over low heat for about 20 minutes. Season with salt and chopped mint.

Prepare the zucchini flowers: Carefully unfurl the flower petals and spoon in 1 tablespoon seasoned goat curd so that it holds its shape. Gently twist the petals to reseal the flower.

Place a rack on the highest shelf of the oven and turn the broiler to its highest setting. When hot, place a greased 10-inch cast-iron pan on the stove, set to medium heat.

Sprinkle a little flour over your hands and on the work surface and open the dough ball by flattening and stretching the dough with your fingers, or by rolling the dough with a rolling pin. Pick the pizza base up and gently stretch it a little more over your fists without tearing it. Drop this onto the hot pan, and allow it to start rising.

As soon as the dough firms up, drizzle with the olive oil. Distribute a quarter of the zucchini evenly over the pizza, then add the basil, Gruyère, and mozzarella.

Cook the pizza on top of the stove for about 3 minutes, then transfer the pan to the broiler for another 3 to 4 minutes.

Finish with a curd-filled zucchini flower and serve whole or in slices.

A Caprese is similar to a Margherita pizza but uses all the ingredients in their raw (and best) states, like a wonderful Tricolore salad.

CAPRESE BAKED

ingredients, per pizza

1 dough ball (see page 16),
   left to rise for
   1¹/₂ to 2 hours
flour, for dusting

2 teaspoons olive oil
¹/₂ teaspoon flaked sea salt
pinch of oregano
3 large, ripe, juicy
   tomatoes, sliced
3 ounces buffalo
   mozzarella, sliced
4 basil leaves, torn
1 tablespoon basil-infused
   olive oil

Place a rack on the highest shelf of the oven and turn the broiler to its highest setting. When hot, place a greased 10-inch cast-iron pan on the stove, set to medium heat.

Sprinkle a little flour over your hands and on the work surface and open the dough ball by flattening and stretching the dough with your fingers, or by rolling the dough with a rolling pin. Pick the pizza base up and gently stretch it a little more over your fists without tearing it. Drop this onto the hot pan, and allow it to start rising.

As soon as the dough firms up, drizzle the olive oil over the base and add the salt and a pinch of oregano.

Cook the pizza on top of the stove for about 3 minutes, then transfer the pan to the broiler for another 3 to 4 minutes.

Arrange the tomato slices, mozzarella, and basil, alternately, in a circle over the base, and drizzle with a little basil-infused olive oil.

Serve whole or in slices.

INGREDIENT NOTE

Basil pesto (see page 34) makes a tasty and decorative addition, but only if you have it— this is a pizza designed for minimum fuss and maximum freshness.
   If you have very good tomatoes, and more time on your hands, try the Positanese recipe on page 119.

Smoked cheese makes an interesting alternative to mozzarella on pizzas, and you can purchase great smoked cheeses from many producers. If you want to try smoking cheese yourself, and you do not have a wood smoker, try tea-smoking in an ordinary domestic oven. We have suggested a way to do this, on page 23.

WILD MUSHROOM &
TEA-SMOKED CHEESE BAKED OR SHEET

ingredients, per pizza

1 dough ball (see page 16),
   left to rise for
   1½ to 2 hours OR
   dough 2 for sheet pizzas
flour, for dusting

for the wild mushrooms
   (makes enough
   for 4 baked pizzas)
6 ounces wild mushrooms
1 tablespoons extra virgin
   olive oil
1 tablespoon butter
pinch of sea salt

2 teaspoons olive oil
1 ounce tea-smoked
   cheese (see page 23)
2 ounces *mozzarella fior di
   latte*, torn into 5 chunks
4 basil leaves, torn

Prepare the wild mushrooms: Rub the mushrooms with a damp towel to remove any dirt. Do not soak them in water or they become slimy. Heat the olive oil and butter in a frying pan over low heat and sear the mushrooms for about 3 minutes, seasoning with a pinch of salt.

Place a rack on the highest shelf of the oven and turn the broiler to its highest setting. When hot, place a greased 10-inch cast-iron pan on the stove, set to medium heat.

Sprinkle a little flour over your hands and on the work surface and open the dough ball by flattening and stretching the dough with your fingers, or by rolling the dough with a rolling pin. Pick the pizza base up and gently stretch it a little more over your fists without tearing it. Drop this onto the hot pan, and allow it to start rising.

As soon as the dough firms up, drizzle the olive oil over the base. Add a quarter of the mushrooms, then scatter the smoked cheese, mozzarella, and basil on top.

Cook the pizza on top of the stove for about 3 minutes, then transfer the pan to the broiler for another 3 to 4 minutes.

Serve whole or in slices.

For the sheet method
Follow the recipe instructions on page 19. The whole process will take about 90 minutes. Heat the oven to 500°F and stretch the dough to the edges of the sheet. Be sure to spread your sauce right to the edges before adding toppings. The sheet pizza dough serves 4, so quadruple the ingredient quantities. Bake for no less than 10 minutes.

The sweet and pleasant flavor of butternut squash pairs well with a light, fresh goat curd. Since this is a simple pizza, it really highlights the quality of your ingredients so make sure you have a good olive oil if possible.

BUTTERNUT SQUASH & GOAT CURD BAKED

ingredients, per pizza

1 dough ball (see page 16),
   left to rise for
   1½ to 2 hours
flour, for dusting

for the butternut squash
   (makes enough
   for 4 baked pizzas)
6 ounces butternut
   squash, peeled and cut
   into small wedges
2 tablespoons olive oil
sea salt

2 teaspoons extra virgin
   olive oil
2 ounces *mozzarella fior di
   latte*, torn into 6 chunks
2 tablespoons goat curd
basil pesto, optional
   (see page 34)

Prepare the butternut squash: Preheat the oven to 425°F.
Coat the wedges in the olive oil, sprinkle with salt and bake in the oven for 40 minutes, turning once. Reduce to 350°F after 20 minutes. By the end, the squash should be a sticky, caramelized, mashed consistency, not hard at all. Set aside.

Place a rack on the highest shelf of the oven and turn the broiler to its highest setting. When hot, place a greased 10-inch cast-iron pan on the stove, set to medium heat.

Sprinkle a little flour over your hands and on the work surface and open the dough ball by flattening and stretching the dough with your fingers, or by rolling the dough with a rolling pin. Pick the pizza base up and gently stretch it a little more over your fists without tearing it. Drop this onto the hot pan, and allow it to start rising.

As soon as the dough firms up, spread the butternut mash onto the pizza with the back of a moistened metal spoon. Drizzle with olive oil and add the mozzarella. Dollop 1 tablespoon of curd around the top of the pizza.

Cook the pizza on top of the stove for about 3 minutes, then transfer the pan to the broiler for another 3 to 4 minutes.

Once ready, dress with the remainder of the curd and some basil pesto, if you like, and serve in pieces or whole.

INGREDIENT NOTE

An alternative method for preparing the butternut squash is to boil it in a little water for 10 to 15 minutes until cooked through. Then transfer to a bowl, add a little butter and salt, and mash.

Spring, and particularly early spring in a southern climate, is the best season for artichokes. Artichoke season does not last long, so eat as much of this delight as you can, while you can.

ARTICHOKES, NEW POTATOES, & SCALLIONS *SHEET*

ingredients, per pizza

1 quantity dough 2
flour, for dusting

**for the vegetable topping
(makes enough
for 4 baked pizzas)**
2 tablespoons olive oil
14 ounces scallions, thinly
   sliced
3 ounces firm, waxy new
   potatoes, sliced ½ inch
   thick
1 large artichoke,
   quartered (see box)
sea salt and freshly ground
   black pepper
several sprigs mint
flat-leaf parsley, chopped

2 tablespoons olive oil
3 ounces *mozzarella fior di
   latte*, torn into 8 chunks
½ cup grated Parmigiano
   reggiano

This is a sheet pizza (see page 19). Turn your oven to its highest setting and place a rack on the middle shelf.

Stretch the dough toward the edges of a 9 × 12-inch oiled baking sheet in 2 stages, resting for 10 minutes between each stretch.

Make the vegetable topping: Heat the oil in a wide, shallow pan and sweat the scallions over very low heat, to soften. Add the potatoes and artichoke quarters and add about ½ cup water. Sprinkle with ½ teaspoon salt, a few grinds of pepper, a few mint leaves and plenty of parsley. Cover and cook for 10 minutes. After 5 minutes, either remove the lid or continue to cook covered, depending on how fast the water is evaporating. Your aim is to cook off all the water.

Pour a little olive oil into the palm of your hand and pat it lightly over the top of the dough, making sure it touches the edges. Add the mozzarella and sprinkle half the Parmesan over the base. Add the artichoke, potato, and onion, distributing it evenly over the pizza.

Bake on the middle rack of your preheated oven for 12–14 minutes. If you have created a very thin pizza base, check for doneness after 10 minutes.

Once ready, sprinkle the remaining Parmesan on top and serve in slices.

INGREDIENT NOTE

To prepare the artichokes, remove the outer leaves and, with a sharp knife, remove the top spike and the hard skin of the stalk. Cut the artichoke lengthwise and remove the choke (too much denotes a bad artichoke), then slice and rest in water with a squeeze of lemon juice to prevent oxidation.

This mix of eggplant, capers, garlic, and pine nuts is also known as a caponata and is an Italian classic. It is well worth making extra because not only does it make a great pizza topping, but it's delicious as a salad or an accompaniment to baked fish.

EGGPLANT WITH CAPERS, ROASTED GARLIC, & PINE NUTS (CAPONATA) BAKED OR FRIED

ingredients, per pizza

1 dough ball (see page 16),
   left to rise for
   1½ to 2 hours
flour, for dusting

for the caponata:
   (makes enough
   for 4 baked pizzas)
1 heaping tablespoon
   capers in salt (or large,
   good-quality capers in
   brine)
4 large garlic cloves,
   whole, unpeeled
4 teaspoons pine nuts
¾ cup extra virgin olive oil
2 large eggplants, cut into
   4 thick slices,
   then cubed
16 basil leaves, torn

1 tablespoon tomato sauce
   (see page 20)
3 basil leaves, torn
2 ounces *mozzarella fior di
   latte*, torn into 5 chunks
olive oil, for drizzling

Make the caponata: Preheat the oven to 400°F. Soak the capers in water for half an hour or so. If using the unsalted variety, simply wash well and dry off.

Roast the garlic in its skin for about 10 minutes, or until soft and brown. Toast the pine nuts in a hot pan, watching carefully that they do not burn. Peel the garlic and reserve. In a small frying pan, warm the oil over low heat and cook the capers for about 10 minutes. Add the eggplant and cook until tender. Take the pan off the heat and add the pine nuts, garlic, and basil. Set aside–the flavors will infuse as the mixture cools.

Place a rack on the highest shelf of the oven and turn the broiler to its highest setting. When hot, place a greased 10-inch cast-iron pan on the stove, set to medium heat.

Sprinkle a little flour over your hands and on the work surface and open the dough ball by flattening and stretching the dough with your fingers, or by rolling the dough with a rolling pin. Pick the pizza base up and gently stretch it a little more over your fists without tearing it. Drop this onto the hot pan, and allow it to start rising.

As soon as the dough firms up, spread the tomato sauce over the base with the back of a metal spoon. Distribute 2 tablespoons of caponata evenly over the top and finish with the basil, mozzarella, and a drizzle of olive oil.

Cook the pizza on top of the stove for about 3 minutes, then transfer the pan to the broiler for another 3 to 4 minutes.

Once ready, serve with an extra spoonful of caponata and chunk of mozzarella on the side.

For fried pizza, see the method on page 17

Ricotta is sometimes in danger of being a little bland (as opposed to subtle). However, the less fat in the milk, the closer the ricotta is to yogurt, giving it an interesting "tang." The best ricotta is usually sheep milk ricotta, followed by buffalo, then cow.

ZUCCHINI & RICOTTA   BAKED OR FRIED

ingredients, per pizza
1 dough ball (see page 16),
    left to rise for
    1½ to 2 hours
flour, for dusting

for the zucchini
    (makes enough
    for 4 baked pizzas)
2 cups thinly sliced
    zucchini
1 tablespoon olive oil
10 basil leaves, torn
5 mint leaves, finely
    chopped

for the *crema di ricotta*:
    (makes enough
    for 1 baked pizza)
2 teaspoons milk
1 tablespoon ricotta
sea salt

2 teaspoons extra virgin
    olive oil
4 basil leaves, torn
2 ounces *mozzarella fior di
    latte*, torn into 5 chunks
1 heaping tablespoon
    grated Pecorino

Prepare the zucchini: Place the zucchini in a wide, shallow pan and stir in the oil and basil. Cook, covered, over low heat for about 20 minutes. Season with salt and chopped mint.

Make the crema di ricotta: In a bowl, stir the milk into the ricotta and mix to a smooth consistency. Season with salt and pepper to taste.

Place a rack on the highest shelf of the oven and turn the broiler to its highest setting. When hot, place a greased 10-inch cast-iron pan on the stove, set to medium heat.

Sprinkle a little flour over your hands and on the work surface and open the dough ball by flattening and stretching the dough with your fingers, or by rolling the dough with a rolling pin. Pick the pizza base up and gently stretch it a little more over your fists without tearing it. Drop this onto the hot pan, and allow it to start rising.

As soon as the dough firms up, spread the *crema di ricotta* over the base with the back of a metal spoon. Drizzle over the olive oil and distribute the zucchinis and basil evenly over the surface. Finish with the mozzarella and grated Pecorino.

Cook the pizza on top of the stove for about 3 minutes, then transfer the pan to the broiler for another 3 to 4 minutes.

Once ready, dress with the remaining Pecorino and serve whole or in slices.

For fried pizza, see the method on page 17

INGREDIENT NOTE

When you buy your zucchini, try to find zucchini flowers at the same time, because you can stuff them with ricotta, wrap them in dough, deep-fry the whole flower, and enjoy as an appetizer.

Chorizo is a strong cured meat with plenty of flavor and spicy aroma. When you contrast this with a fresh, mild cheese such as ricotta, and throw in plenty of crunchy green watercress to balance it, you are in no danger of adulterating its deep umami.

CHORIZO WITH RICOTTA & WATERCRESS BAKED

ingredients, per pizza

1 dough ball (see page 16),
   left to rise for
   1½ to 2 hours
flour, for dusting

for the *crema di ricotta*:
   (makes enough
   for 1 baked pizza)
2 teaspoons milk
1 heaping tablespoon
   ricotta
sea salt

2 teaspoons extra virgin
   olive oil
6 slices chorizo
6 chunks cooking chorizo,
   skinned and broken
2 ounces *mozzarella fior di
   latte*, torn into 5 chunks
4 basil leaves, torn
a small handful of
   watercress, washed
   and dried

Make the crema di ricotta: In a bowl, stir the milk into the ricotta and mix to a smooth consistency. Season with salt and pepper to taste.

Place a rack on the highest shelf of the oven and turn the broiler to its highest setting. When hot, place a greased 10-inch cast-iron pan on the stove, set to medium heat.

Sprinkle a little flour over your hands and on the work surface and open the dough ball by flattening and stretching the dough with your fingers, or by rolling the dough with a rolling pin. Pick the pizza base up and gently stretch it a little more over your fists without tearing it. Drop this onto the hot pan, and allow it to start rising.

As soon as the dough firms up, turn the heat down to medium and drizzle with the olive oil. Spread the *crema di ricotta* over the base with the back of a metal spoon. Add both types of chorizo and the mozzarella and distribute the basil leaves on top.

Cook the pizza on top of the stove for about 3 minutes, then transfer the pan to the broiler for another 3 to 4 minutes.

Once ready, finish with a mound of watercress. Serve whole.

Italians appreciate and take great pride in the authentic flavors of their respective regions. They celebrate the fruits of their various terroirs by producing wines, cheeses, and diverse regional products, many of which have acquired international renown.

Capers, olives, and anchovies are crucial to the gastronomy of Southern Italy. Around Naples, where the iconic *Pizza Alla Napoletana* was born, these three ingredients feature significantly, both together and apart, in many signature dishes and recipes.

NEOPOLITAN BAKED OR FRIED

ingredients, per pizza

1 dough ball (see page 16),
   left to rise for
   1 1/2 to 2 hours
flour, for dusting

8 capers in salt
1 garlic clove, peeled and
   roughly chopped
2 tablespoons olive oil
1 tablespoon tomato sauce
   (see page 20)
1 teaspoon oregano
4 anchovy fillets
5 Kalamata olives, a
   mixture of black
   and green
4 basil leaves, torn (plus
   more to serve)
2 ounces *mozzarella fior di
latte*, torn into 5 chunks

Wash the salted capers and soak them in plenty of water for at least 1 hour, then drain.

Cook the garlic in 1 tablespoon of the olive oil until lightly golden, then stir in the tomato sauce.

Place a rack on the highest shelf of the oven and turn the broiler to its highest setting. When hot, place a greased 10-inch cast-iron pan on the stove, set to medium heat.

Sprinkle a little flour over your hands and on the work surface and open the dough ball by flattening and stretching the dough with your fingers, or by rolling the dough with a rolling pin. Pick the pizza base up and gently stretch it a little more over your fists without tearing it. Drop this onto the hot pan, and allow it to start rising.

As soon as the dough firms up in the hot pan, spread the tomato and garlic sauce over the base with the back of a metal spoon. Sprinkle over the oregano and the remaining olive oil.

Distribute the anchovies, olives, capers, and basil leaves evenly over the surface and scatter the cheese on top.

Cook the pizza on top of the stove for about 3 minutes, then transfer the pan to the broiler for another 3 to 4 minutes.

Once ready, decorate with more basil and serve in one piece or sliced.

For fried pizza, see the method on page 17

This is a lovely vegetarian pizza that enhances a signature vegetable (spinach) with the simple addition of butter and a good, sharp cheese.

SPINACH, BUTTER, & PECORINO BAKED

ingredients, per pizza

1 dough ball (see page 16),
　　left to rise for
　　1½ to 2 hours
flour, for dusting

**for the spinach
　(makes enough
　for 4 baked pizzas)**
2 teaspoons extra virgin
　　olive oil
1 garlic clove, crushed
9 ounces spinach
sea salt and freshly ground
　　black pepper

**for the *crema di ricotta*
　(makes enough
　for 1 baked pizza)**
2 teaspoons milk
1 heaping tablespoon
　　ricotta
sea salt

2 teaspoons extra virgin
　　olive oil
2 ounces *mozzarella fior di
　latte*, torn into 5 chunks
a few dots of butter
1 heaping tablespoon
　　grated Pecorino

Prepare the spinach: Heat the oil in a wide, shallow pan and cook the garlic. Add the spinach, some salt, and a drop of water, and cover. Cook for about 4 minutes. Drain well and squeeze excess water from the leaves before using.

Make the crema di ricotta: In a bowl, stir the milk into the ricotta and mix to a smooth consistency. Season with salt and pepper to taste.

Place a rack on the highest shelf of the oven and turn the broiler to its highest setting. When hot, place a greased 10-inch cast-iron pan on the stove, set to medium heat.

Sprinkle a little flour over your hands and on the work surface and open the dough ball by flattening and stretching the dough with your fingers, or by rolling the dough with a rolling pin. Pick the pizza base up and gently stretch it a little more over your fists without tearing it. Drop this onto the hot pan, and allow it to start rising.

As soon as the dough firms up, spread the *crema di ricotta* over the base using the back of a metal spoon. Drizzle over the olive oil, and add the spinach and mozzarella.

Cook the pizza on top of the stove for about 3 minutes, then transfer the pan to the broiler for another 3 to 4 minutes.

Once ready, drop dots of soft butter onto the pizza and sprinkle the grated Pecorino on top. Serve whole or in slices.

Look for a pancetta that has been rolled in mountain herbs because these add an extra dimension of flavor. Bacon will do but definitely takes second place to a well-produced sweet pancetta. Or you could leave out the meat altogether, because spinach, olives, and smoked mozzarella make a lovely vegetarian option.

PANCETTA, SPINACH, OLIVES, & SMOKED CHEESE BAKED

ingredients, per pizza

1 dough ball (see page 16), left to rise for 1¹/₂ to 2 hours
flour, for dusting

for the spinach (makes enough for 1 baked pizza)
2 teaspoons extra virgin olive oil
1 garlic clove, crushed
¹/₂ red chile, finely chopped (optional)
9 ounces spinach
sea salt

2 teaspoons extra virgin olive oil
4 Kalamata olives
2 ounces *mozzarella fior di latte*, torn into 5 chunks
1 ounce smoked buffalo mozzarella, torn into 3 chunks
4 slices pancetta
Pecorino or Parmesan, to serve

Prepare the spinach: Heat a little oil in a pan and cook the chile and garlic. Add the spinach, some salt, and a drop of water and cover. Cook for about 4 minutes. Drain well and squeeze excess water from the leaves before using.

Place a rack on the highest shelf of the oven and turn the broiler to its highest setting. When hot, place a greased 10-inch cast-iron pan on the stove, set to medium heat.

Sprinkle a little flour over your hands and on the work surface and open the dough ball by flattening and stretching the dough with your fingers, or by rolling the dough with a rolling pin. Pick the pizza base up and gently stretch it a little more over your fists without tearing it. Drop this onto the hot pan, and allow it to start rising.

As soon as the dough firms up, drizzle with the olive oil. Spread the spinach over the base and add the olives, both types of mozzarella, and the pancetta.

Cook the pizza on top of the stove for about 3 minutes, then transfer the pan to the broiler for another 3 to 4 minutes.

Once ready, sprinkle with fresh shavings of Parmesan or Pecorino and serve whole or in slices

INGREDIENT NOTE

Black olives are better than green for pizza, or a mix for Puttanesca (see page 109). Green olives are picked earlier (before ripening) and are generally firmer—better for eating fresh, or in salads. We particularly like the meaty flavor of Kalamata olives.

Although a little difficult to prepare, the artichoke heart really is the heart of the matter, and its rich, creamy texture needs only a little fresh mozzarella and olive oil to set it off. However, the potent tomato addition here delivers that extra deep, sundried flavor and brings all the elements in this pizza together.

ARTICHOKE, WITH SUNDRIED TOMATOES, PARMESAN, & BUFFALO MOZZARELLA   BAKED

ingredients, per pizza

1 dough ball (see page 16),
   left to rise for
   1¹/₂ to 2 hours
flour, for dusting

2 teaspoons extra virgin
   olive oil
3 sundried tomatoes,
   sliced
1 artichoke heart,
   quartered
4 teaspoons grated
   Parmesan
2 ounces buffalo
   mozzarella, torn into
   5 chunks
sea salt and freshly ground
   black pepper

Place a rack on the highest shelf of the oven and turn the broiler to its highest setting. When hot, place a greased 10-inch cast-iron pan on the stove, set to medium heat.

Sprinkle a little flour over your hands and on the work surface and open the dough ball by flattening and stretching the dough with your fingers, or by rolling the dough with a rolling pin. Pick the pizza base up and gently stretch it a little more over your fists without tearing it. Drop this onto the hot pan, and allow it to start rising.

As soon as the dough firms up, drizzle the base with olive oil and lay the sundried tomatoes and artichoke on top. Sprinkle with half the Parmesan cheese.

Cook the pizza on top of the stove for about 3 minutes, then transfer the pan to the broiler for another 3 to 4 minutes.

Once ready, finish with mounds of fresh buffalo mozzarella, season, and finish with the remaining Parmesan.

INGREDIENT NOTE

See page 93 for how to prepare artichokes. However, if you want to save time, grilled artichokes bottled in oil are a perfectly fine alternative.

As with all ham products, it is best to choose the fattier cuts and varieties, as the thinly sliced fats melt easily and moisten the pizza dough. This is especially tasty on a bianca pizza, where there's no tomato sauce.

PROSCIUTTO, PECORINO, & ARUGULA   BAKED

ingredients, per pizza

1 dough ball (see page 16), left to rise for 1½ to 2 hours
flour, for dusting

2 teaspoons extra virgin olive oil
4 to 5 cherry tomatoes, halved
1 teaspoon sea salt
2 ounces *mozzarella fior di latte*, torn into 5 chunks
4 slices Senese ham (or Prosciutto)
1 heaping tablespoon Pecorino, grated
2 ounces buffalo mozzarella, torn into 4 chunks (optional)
a handful of arugula

Place a rack on the highest shelf of the oven and turn the broiler to its highest setting. When hot, place a greased 10-inch cast-iron pan on the stove, set to medium heat.

Sprinkle the salt over the cherry tomatoes and set aside.

Sprinkle a little flour over your hands and on the work surface and open the dough ball by flattening and stretching the dough with your fingers, or by rolling the dough with a rolling pin. Pick the pizza base up and gently stretch it a little more over your fists without tearing it. Drop this onto the hot pan, and allow it to start rising.

As soon as the dough firms up, drizzle the base with olive oil. Lay the cherry tomatoes face down, then add the mozzarella and ham slices on top and sprinkle with half the Pecorino.

Cook the pizza on top of the stove for about 3 minutes, then transfer the pan to the broiler for another 3 to 4 minutes.

Finish with mounds of fresh buffalo mozzarella and a handful of arugula leaves, and sprinkle with the remaining Pecorino.

This recipe is a nod to the classic pasta sauce traditionally served with spaghetti, which takes advantage of fresh summer tomatoes and Italy's all-year signature ingredients: olives, capers, and garlic.

PUTTANESCA BAKED OR SHEET

ingredients, per pizza

1 dough ball (see page 16),
   left to rise for
   1½ to 2 hours OR
   dough 2 for sheet pizzas
flour, for dusting

for the salsa
   (makes enough
   for 8 baked pizzas)
3 fresh tomatoes
1 teaspoon salt
1 garlic clove, crushed
4 basil leaves, chopped

1 heaping tablespoon
   salted capers
2 tablespoons olive oil
½ garlic clove, finely
   chopped
chile, finely sliced
6 to 8 black and green
   olives, pitted and
   chopped
3 ounces *mozzarella fior di
   latte*, torn into 6 chunks
½ teaspoon dried oregano
3 basil leaves, torn
freshly ground black
   pepper

Make the salsa: Soak the salted capers in plenty of water for at least 1 hour, then drain. Place the tomatoes in a pot of boiling water, remove from the stove, and leave for about 3 minutes. Peel, seed, and finely chop the tomatoes, then transfer to a sieve, salt, and drain for about 20 minutes. Transfer the tomatoes to a bowl with the garlic and basil.

In a saucepan, over low heat, cook the garlic, chile, capers, and olives in 1 tablespoon olive oil, until the garlic starts to brown. Keep warm.

Place a rack on the highest shelf of the oven and turn the broiler to its highest setting. When hot, place a greased 10-inch cast-iron pan on the stove, set to medium heat.

Sprinkle a little flour over your hands and on the work surface and open the dough ball by flattening and stretching the dough with your fingers, or by rolling the dough with a rolling pin. Pick the pizza base up and gently stretch it a little more over your fists without tearing it. Drop this onto the hot pan, and allow it to start rising.

As soon as the dough firms up, spread half the tomato salsa over the base with the back of a metal spoon. Add the mozzarella, a sprinkle of oregano and a drizzle of olive oil.

Cook the pizza on top of the stove for about 3 minutes, then transfer the pan to the broiler for another 3 to 4 minutes.

Combine the rest of the tomatoes with the pan-fried mixture and some basil. Add to the baked pizza when it comes out the oven with a grind or two of black pepper. Serve whole or in slices.

For the sheet method

Follow the recipe instructions on page 19. The whole process will take about 90 minutes. Heat the oven to 500°F and stretch the dough to the edges of the baking sheet. Be sure to spread your sauce right to the edges before adding toppings. The sheet pizza dough serves 4, so quadruple the ingredient quantities. Bake for no less than 10 minutes.

There is, arguably, nothing better than fresh asparagus spears bursting with moisture and earthy seasonal flavor. Together with fresh mozzarella and the purity of the best Parmesan reggiano, this simple pizza is a spring treat.

ASPARAGUS & BUFFALO MOZZARELLA BAKED

ingredients, per pizza

1 dough ball (see page 16), left to rise for 1½ to 2 hours
flour, for dusting

12 asparagus spears, trimmed
2 teaspoons extra virgin olive oil
2 ounces *mozzarella fior di latte*, torn into 5 chunks
a few dots of butter
2 ounces buffalo mozzarella, torn into 5 chunks
Parmesan shavings
a few basil leaves, torn

Place a rack on the highest shelf of the oven and turn the broiler to its highest setting. When hot, place a greased 10-inch cast-iron pan on the stove, set to medium heat.

Bring a little water to a boil in a wide-bottomed pan, then steam the asparagus for a couple of minutes. A lid will help this along more thoroughly, but otherwise turn them once, then drain.

Sprinkle a little flour over your hands and on the work surface and open the dough ball by flattening and stretching the dough with your fingers, or by rolling the dough with a rolling pin. Pick the pizza base up and gently stretch it a little more over your fists without tearing it. Drop this onto the hot pan, and allow it to start rising.

As soon as the dough firms up, drizzle the olive oil over the base. Lay the asparagus over the pizza and distribute the mozzarella evenly.

Cook the pizza on top of the stove for about 3 minutes, then transfer the pan to the broiler for another 3 to 4 minutes.

Dress the pizza with a little butter, the bufffalo mozzarella, and a few Parmesan shavings and torn basil leaves. Serve whole or in slices.

INGREDIENT NOTE
- - - - - - - - - - - - - -
Divide the dough into smaller balls to make two little pizzas, as pictured, or any size you prefer.

Leeks go very well with potatoes, and Cheddar cheese works well with both. This pizza is designed to have a full flavor, taking advantage of ingredients that combine beautifully.

LEEK, POTATO, & CHEDDAR   *SHEET*

1 quantity sheet dough
flour, for dusting

for the vegetable topping
2 tablespoons unsalted
    butter
4 cups thinly sliced
    scallions
1/3 cup thinly sliced onion
4 cups thinly sliced leeks
1/2 cup potatoes, sliced
    thinly
freshly ground black
    pepper

1 tablespoon olive oil
2 ounces *mozzarella fior di
    latte*, sliced
3/4 cup grated extra
    mature Cheddar
a few sprigs of flat-leaf
    parsley, chopped

This is a sheet pizza (see page 19). Turn your oven to its highest setting and place a rack on the middle shelf.

Stretch the dough toward the edges of a 9 × 12-inch oiled baking sheet in 2 stages, resting for 10 minutes between each stretch.

Make the vegetable topping: Melt the butter in a wide-bottomed pan over very low heat and sweat the scallions and leeks until tender– avoid browning. Add the potatoes and 1/2 cup water, then cover and cook for 10 minutes. After 5 minutes, either remove the lid or continue to cook covered, depending on how fast the water is evaporating. Your aim is to cook off all the water.

Pour a little olive oil into the palm of your hand and pat it lightly over the top of the dough, making sure it touches the edges. Add the sliced mozzarella and the onion and potato mixture, and spread the Cheddar on top.

Bake on the middle rack of your preheated oven for about 10 minutes. If you have created a very thin pizza base, check for doneness after 10 minutes.

Once ready, decorate with a little chopped parsley and serve in 4 slices.

ROSEMARY & SEA SALT FOCCACCIA

An unadulterated sheet pizza (without tomato, cheese, or other meats and vegetables) makes a great bread for the table or for sandwiches. Use a smaller sheet, so you increase the height of the dough.

1 quantity sheet dough (see page 19)
2 teaspoons olive oil
sea salt, crushed
1 branch rosemary, sprigs removed

Turn your oven on to its highest setting. Follow the method for the sheet pizza dough on page 19, and start with your dough stretched out to meet the sides of an oiled baking sheet.

Pour the olive oil into the palm of your hand and pat it lightly over the top of the dough, making sure it touches the edges. Dimple the dough with your fingertips and add a little more oil. Sprinkle the crushed sea salt on top and gently push the rosemary into the dimples, without degassing the dough in too many places. (You can also mix slightly roasted, crushed rosemary into the dough beforehand and just finish with salt and olive oil.)

Bake in the oven for 8 to 10 minutes. Once ready, leave to cool. This can be served as a fresh bread, or left to stale slightly and used for bruschette.

BRUSCHETTA

Slice the focaccia (see method above) into desired lengths about ½ inch wide. Toast and add toppings of your choice. All of the sheet-baked pizza toppings can also be used for bruschetta but here are a few more ideas:

Garlic butter—Mash a few cloves of fresh garlic with softened butter and a few sprigs of chopped parsley and spread onto the bruschetta while hot.

Napoletana—Finely chop a mix of capers, olives, and anchovies to make a salty tapenade and spread on hot bruschetta.

Pesto—See page 34.

These pizzette make a fresh and colorful summer treat since the toppings are all added after the dough has been fried. Also, because they're quick and simple to prepare, they make excellent canapés.

PIZZETTE *FRIED*

**ingredients, (makes
8 canape pizzas or
16 pizzette)**

1 quantity dough 1
   (see page 17)
flour, for dusting

$^3/_4$ cup tomato sauce
   (see page 20)
$^3/_4$ cup groundnut or
   vegetable oil
8 ounces *mozzarella
   fior di latte* or buffalo
   mozzarella, torn into
   small chunks
$^3/_4$ cup grated Parmesan
10 basil leaves, shredded
sea salt and freshly ground
   black pepper

Divide the dough into 8 or 16 pieces (depending on whether you want to make canape pizzas or pizzette). Shape these into round balls, cover, and leave to rise for an hour in a warm place.

Simmer the tomato sauce over low heat to reduce for about 6 minutes. (This is important to enhance the flavor because the sauce is not cooked with the dough). Keep warm.

Sprinkle a little flour over your hands and on the work surface and open the dough balls by flattening and stretching the dough with your fingers, or by rolling the dough with a rolling pin.

Heat the oil in a deep, wide saucepan on a medium heat.

Gently, without tearing, stretch the dough with your fingertips. Drop this onto the hot oil, and allow to start rising. Turn the heat down if necessary—do not brown the pizzette, they should be golden. In batches, fry for a couple of minutes, turning once or twice.

Add the mozzarella, a sprinkle of Parmesan, and a basil garnish, and then top with the hot tomato sauce and season to taste.

Other recipes we recommend you use for pizzette can be found on pages 32, 72, 94, 97 and 101.

This raw salsa is a classic from Positano on the Amalfi coast. You need very good tomatoes for this, so make sure that you find some that are super-sweet and fruity. We also call this pizza "a la Eduardo," a reference to Eduardo di Filippo, the famous Italian actor, playwright, author, and poet, who passed this recipe on to us many years ago.

POSITANESE BAKED

ingredients, per pizza

1 dough ball (see page 16), left to rise for 1½ to 2 hours

flour, for dusting

for the salsa
(makes enough for 4 pizzas)

2 medium tomatoes

½ teaspoon salt

1 garlic clove, crushed

½ tablespoon mashed onion

2 tablespoons olive oil

4 basil leaves

a pinch of dried oregano

a pinch of marjoram

a few sprigs of fresh parsley, chopped

1 tablespoon chopped celery

freshly ground black pepper

Parmesan, grated

Make the salsa: Bring a pot of water to a boil and remove from the stove. Place the tomatoes in the water and leave for about 3 minutes until their skins start to wrinkle. Peel and seed the tomatoes and finely chop.

Place the tomatoes in a sieve, add the salt, and leave to drain over a bowl for about 20 minutes. Discard the juice and transfer the drained tomatoes to a large bowl with the garlic.

Add all the remaining salsa ingredients and stir to combine. Marinate for at least 2 hours (it will keep in the fridge for up to 2 days, although if you do this, bring it up to room temperature before use).

Place a rack on the highest shelf of the oven and turn the broiler to its highest setting. When hot, place a greased 10-inch cast-iron pan on the stove, set to medium heat.

Divide the salsa into two bowls and set one aside, reserving it for later (in total, ensure you have enough for about 4 tablespoons per pizza).

Sprinkle a little flour over your hands and on the work surface and open the dough ball by flattening and stretching the dough with your fingers, or by rolling the dough with a rolling pin. Pick the pizza base up and gently stretch it a little more over your fists without tearing it. Drop this onto the hot pan, and allow it to start rising.

As soon as the dough firms up, spread a quarter of the tomato salsa over the base with the back of a metal spoon.

Cook the pizza on top of the stove for about 3 minutes, then transfer the pan to the broiler for another 3 to 4 minutes.

Once ready, add 2 tablespoons of the reserved salsa (at room temperature) and finish with Parmesan, either grated or shaved, with extra basil if you like. Serve whole or in slices.

The radicchio is essential to this recipe as its wonderful bitterness perfectly offsets the fatty sweetness of the guanciale. It retains some texture, too, so its crunch also offsets the cheese. Our favorite kinds of radicchio are the *Treviggiana* varieties, from the Treviso area of Italy. These can be roasted or broiled until caramelized.

RADDICCHIO, SMOKED
MOZZARELLA, & GUANCIALE BAKED

ingredients, per pizza

1 dough ball (see page 16),
    left to rise for
    1½ to 2 hours
flour, for dusting

for the radicchio
    (makes enough
    for 4 pizzas)

4 ounces (about 24
    leaves) radicchio leaves
    (preferably Treviggiana)
2 tablespoons extra virgin
    olive oil
generous pinch of salt

2 teaspoons extra virgin
    olive oil (or lard)
4 slices guanciale, sliced
4 basil leaves, torn
1 ounce smoked
    mozzarella, torn into
    4 chunks
4 teaspoons grated
    Parmesan
sea salt and freshly ground
    black pepper
2 ounces buffalo
    mozzarella, torn into
    5 chunks

Prepare the radicchio: In a large bowl, mix the radicchio with the olive oil and salt and leave to marinate for 40 minutes.

Place a rack on the highest shelf of the oven and turn the broiler to its highest setting. When hot, place a greased 10-inch cast-iron pan on the stove, set to medium heat.

Sprinkle a little flour over your hands and on the work surface and open the dough ball by flattening and stretching the dough with your fingers, or by rolling the dough with a rolling pin. Pick the pizza base up and gently stretch it a little more over your fists without tearing it. Drop this onto the hot pan, and allow it to start rising.

As soon as the dough firms up, drizzle on the olive oil. Arrange the guanciale on top, then add the radicchio, basil, and smoked mozzarella. Scatter half the Parmesan on top.

Cook the pizza on top of the stove for about 3 minutes, then transfer the pan to the broiler for another 3 to 4 minutes.

Once ready, finish with a few clumps of the fresh, soft buffalo mozzarella, then season and sprinkle with the remaining Parmesan.

THE SEASONS

If buying ingredients can be fun, growing your own produce is even more rewarding. It also puts you in touch with the seasons and allows recipes to be determined by what is at its peak, in terms of juiciness, color, texture, and flavor and therefore often enhances the quality and the experience. Get into it!

HERBS

ERBE

Herbs are very easy to grow in pots and are fundamental ingredients to have on hand to add that extra fresh dimension to your cooking. For good seed suppliers, see the Resources section.

Arugula

Arugula, or *muralis*, is traditionally collected from the wild—it grows in wall cracks (where lizards help carry the seeds). However, it can also be cultivated and simply requires plenty of drainage and good sun.

Basil

Basil is considered, correctly, an essential ingredient for pizza. The best basil to use is sweet *Ocimum Basilicum* "Napoletano" or "Lettuce Leaf Basil," though *Ocimum minimum* or "Greek Basil" is another good choice. Basil grows well in pots—it likes a sunny window or greenhouse—and adapts to most soils, though it is prone to slug and snail attacks.

Flat-Leaf Parsley

Parsley is a very versatile plant to have to hand and is pretty hardy in most climates. We recommend "Japanese Parsley" for its distinctive flavor with strong hints of celery. It's a perennial so won't need to be replanted. You can also add the roots and young stems to salads. It grows well in the shade but does not like hot weather.

Oregano

Oregano vulgare is a hardy plant and well worth growing. It's also worth looking out for Cretan oregano seeds. This is a very small plant that grows in the high Cretan mountains and can withstand freezing temperatures, but does not like too much water. Plant in a very well-drained soil in full sun.

Mint

Mint is a great, all-year herb and the noninvasive varieties grow well in pots. It goes particularly well with zucchini and lamb pizza toppings and, of course, in almost any kind of salad.

TOMATOES

POMODORI

Tomatoes are also good to grow since industrially farmed types are often lacking in flavor. The best kind are the "heirloom" or "heritage" varieties that have been cultivated over several generations for particular characteristics. We recommend the early-ripening, cold-tolerant "Stupice," which does not even need training, and also the beautiful bright red "Zapotec," which hates cold weather. The oddly named "Orange Banana" is also worth growing because in some areas it can produce fruit well into the autumn and makes a tasty, orangey passata.

VEGETABLES

VERDURE

Our pizza recipes make the most of a wide range of vegetables so if you have a garden to grow your own produce, it's well worth the effort. Here is a breakdown of the pizzas by season so you know what to grow (and what to eat) when:

SPRING *asparagus, leek, potato, spinach, artichoke*

pesto with baked potato & parmesan p. 33
spinach, caramelized onion, goat cheese, & blue cheese p. 61
smoked mozzarella, baked potato & guanciale p. 66
artichokes, new potatoes, & scallions p. 93
spinach, butter, & pecorino p. 102
pancetta, spinach, olives, & smoked cheese p. 105
artichoke, with sundried tomatoes, parmesan, & buffalo mozzarella p. 107
asparagus & buffalo mozzarella p. 110
leek, potato, & cheddar p. 113

SUMMER *zucchini, eggplant, cherry tomato*

bresaola, cherry tomatoes, & buffalo mozzarella p. 29
pancetta & eggplant p. 31
scorched red & yellow peppers p. 52
pork sausage, roasted peppers, & parmesan p. 58
salami, smoked buffalo cheese, & cherry tomatoes p. 65
zucchini, gruyère, & goat curd p. 86
caprese p. 87
eggplant with capers, roasted garlic, & pine nuts p. 94
zucchini & ricotta p. 97
positanese p. 119

AUTUMN *wild mushroom, pepper, butternut squash*

ham, mushroom, & ricotta p. 42
wild mushroom p. 72
wild mushroom & tea-smoked cheese p. 88
butternut squash & goat curd p. 91

WINTER *pumpkin, broccoli/ turnip tops, radicchio*

broccoli, olive, & smoked mozzarella p. 45
treviggiana reggiano, blue cheese, & radicchio p. 53
sausage with wild broccoli p. 55
blue cheese, butternut squash, & pine nuts p. 64
radicchio, caramelized onion, goat cheese, & blue cheese p. 73
mixed cheese with radicchio p. 72
raddicchio, smoked mozzarella, & guanciale p. 121

RESOURCES

Franco Manca

Our chain of pizza restaurants. There are currently 33 branches throughout London, with more on the way. There are several outside of London, too.

www.francomanca.com

LONDON

ALDWYCH

BALHAM

BELSIZE PARK

BERMONDSEY

BRIXTON

BROADGATE CIRCLE

BROADWAY MARKET

BROMLEY

CANARY WHARF

CHISWICK

COVENT GARDEN

ISLINGTON

KENTISH TOWN

KILBURN

KING'S CROSS

MUSWELL HILL

EALING

EARL'S COURT

EAST DULWICH

NORTHCOTE ROAD

RICHMOND

RUSSELL SQUARE

SOHO

SOUTHFIELDS

SOUTH KENSINGTON

STOKE NEWINGTON

TOOTING MARKET

TOTTENHAM COURT ROAD

VICTORIA NOVA

WESTBOURNE GROVE

WESTFIELD LONDON

WESTFIELD STRATFORD

WIMBLEDON

OUTSIDE LONDON

BATH

BOURNEMOUTH

BRIGHTON

BRISTOL

CAMBRIDGE

GUILDFORD

OXFORD

READING

SOUTHAMPTON

ITALY

SALINA

SUPPLIERS

Amazon.com

An excellent source for many ingredients.
www.amazon.com

Dean & Deluca

A great source for vinegars, cheeses, cured meats,
olives, olive oil, and spices.
www.deandeluca.com

The Cook's Garden

A source for plants as well as seeds, some organic.
www.cooksgarden.com

FG Pizza & Italian

A family owned-business specializing in Italian foods
and products, offering a wide assortment of pizza
making supplies.
www.fgpizza.com

Formaggio Kitchen

Will hand-select and ship a wide selection of cheeses,
charcuterie, oils, vinegars, and olives.
www.formaggiokitchen.com

Giusto's Specialty Foods

The leading processor and wholesaler of organically
grown grains. A great souce for specialty flours.
www.giustos.com

Johnny's Selected Seeds

A wide variety of seeds for fruits and vegetables,
including heirloom varieties. The Growing Center
section of the website offers useful tips.
www.johnnyseeds.com

Lodge Cast Iron

A US manufacturer of cast-iron cookware, including
cast-iron frying pans ideal for making pizza.
www.lodgemfg.com

Manicaretti

An importer of artisan-produced Italian foods,
including a wide variety of capers and herbs and
spices.
www.manicaretti.com

The Sausage Maker

Supplier of a wide variety of meat curing products
and natural sausage casings in different sizes,
including beef bung casings.
www.sausagemaker.com

INDEX

A

anchovy 100–1, 114
artichoke
  new potato & scallion 92–3
  sundried tomato, Parmesan &
    buffalo mozzarella 106–7
arugula 32, 122
  bacon & sweet green chile 50–1
  prosciutto ham & Pecorino 108
  & Parmesan salad 48–9
asparagus, & buffalo mozzarella 110–11

B

bacon, sweet green chile & arugula
  50–1
basil 28, 38–9, 87, 100–1, 116–17, 122
  pesto 34–5
beef
  Italian air-cured 71
  Italian meatballs 46–7
blue cheese 78–9
  pancetta & caramelized onion 76–7
  bresaola 71
  butternut squash & pine nut 62–4
  cherry tomato & buffalo mozzarella
    29
  radicchio & Reggiana 53
  spinach, caramelized onion & goat
    cheese 61
brining 57
broccoli
  olive & smoked mozzarella 44–5
  rabe, & sausage 54–5
bruschetta 114
burrata a pugliese 32
butternut squash
  & goat curd 90–1
  pine nut & blue cheese 62–4

C

caper(s) 94–5, 100–1, 109, 114
caponata 94–5
Caprese 87
Cheddar, leek & potato 112–13
cheese 22–3
  mixed, & radicchio 78–9
  see also specific cheeses
chile 50–1
  oil 80
  paste 80

chorizo 74–5
  ricotta & watercress 98–9
curing 68

D

dough 12–19
  bake & fried dough 14–15
  baking in an iron pan 17
  frying 17
  shaping balls 16
  sheet dough 19
  stone baking 17

E

eggplant
  caper, roasted garlic & pine nut 94–5
  & pancetta 30–1
equipment 10–11

F

fats 23
fermentation 13
flour 12
focaccia, rosemary, & sea salt 114
frying dough 17

G

garlic 94–5
  butter 114
goat cheese 78–9
  blue cheese, spinach & caramelized
    onion 61
goat curd
  & butternut squash 90–1
  & salami 82–3
  zucchini & Gruyère 84–6
Gruyère 23
  goat curd & zucchini 84–6
guanciale 70
  radicchio & smoked mozzarella 120–1
  smoked mozzarella & baked potato
    66–7

H

ham
  brining 57
  mushroom & ricotta 42
  Prosciutto, Pecorino & arugula 108
herbs 122

I

iron pan 11

L

lamb
  ground, & Pecorino 36–7
  spicy, mozzarella & tomato 60
lard
  cured 71
  rendering 23
leek, potato & Cheddar 112–13

M

margherita 28
marinara 38–9
meatballs, Italian 46–7
mint 122
mozzarella 22, 28, 32, 60, 73, 78–9,
  100–1, 109, 116–17
  buffalo 29, 87, 106–7, 110–11
  smoked 23, 44–5, 66–7, 120–1
  smoked buffalo 65
mushroom
  field, Pecorino & sausage 43
  ricotta & ham 42
  wild 72
  wild & tea-smoked cheese 88–9
mustard & honey vinaigrette 48–9

N

napoletana bruschetta 114
Neopolitan 100–1

O

oil 23
  chile 80
  olive 44–5, 100–1, 104–5, 109, 114
olive oil 23
onion, caramelized
  blue cheese & pancetta 76–7
  goat cheese, blue cheese &
    spinach 61
  mozzarella, Pecorino & radicchio 73
oregano 38–9, 122

P

pancetta
  & eggplant 30–1

caramelized onion & blue cheese 76–7

spinach, olive, & smoked cheese 104–5

Parmesan 22, 116–17

  baked potato & pesto 33

  buffalo mozzarella, artichoke, & sundried tomato 106–7

  pork sausage & roasted peppers 58–9

  & arugula salad 48–9

passata 20

Pecorino

  & ground lamb 36–7

  arugula & prosciutto 108

  radicchio, caramelized onion & mozzarella 73

  sausage & field mushroom 43

  spinach & butter 102–3

pepper

  caper & garlic 58–9

  roasted, pork sausage & Parmesan 58–9

  scorched red & yellow 52

pesto

  baked potato & Parmesan 33

  basil 34–5

  wild garlic 34

pine nut 62–4, 94–5

pizza stone 11

pizzette 116–17

poolish 19

pork

  DIY sausage 56

  sausage, roasted pepper & Parmesan 58–9

positanese 118–19

potato

  baked, Parmesan & pesto 33

  baked, guanciale & smoked mozzarella 66–7

  Cheddar & leek 112–13

  new, scallion, & artichoke 92–3

puttanesca 109

R

radicchio

  caramelized onion, mozzarella & Pecorino 73

  & mixed cheese 78–9

smoked mozzarella & guanciale 120–1

Reggiano, blue cheese & radicchio 53

ricotta 22

  & zucchini 96–7

  crema di ricotta 22, 42, 72, 96–9, 102–3

  ham & mushroom 42

  watercress & chorizo 98–9

Roquefort 22–3

rosemary & sea salt focaccia 114

S

salad

  arugula & Parmesan 48–9

  mixed leaf 48–9

  salami 68

  & goat curd 82–3

  smoked buffalo cheese & cherry tomato 65

  spicy Calabrian 69

salsa 52, 109, 119

  basic 20

  lardiata (con sugna) 21

salt 12

sausage

  DIY 56

  field mushroom & Pecorino 43

  pork, roasted pepper & Parmesan 58–9

  & broccoli rabe 54–5

seasonal produce 122–3

sheet-baked dough 18–19

smoked cheese 23, 104–5

  buffalo 65

  mozzarella 23, 44–5, 65–7, 120–1

  tea-smoked 88–9

sourdough 12, 13, 14

  starter 12–13

spinach

  butter & Pecorino 102–3

  caramelized onion, goat cheese & blue cheese 61

  olive, smoked cheese, & pancetta 104–5

scallion, artichoke, & new potato 92–3

starters 12

stone baking 17

T

tea-smoked cheese & wild mushroom 88–9

tomato 20–1, 87, 123

  cherry, burrata a pugliese 32

  cherry, buffalo mozzarella & bresaola 29

  cherry, salami & smoked buffalo cheese 65

  salsa 20–1, 52, 109, 119

  sauce 28, 38–9, 116–17

  spicy lamb & mozzarella 60

  sundried, Parmesan, buffalo mozzarella & artichoke 106–7

V

veal, meatballs 46–7

vegetables 123

vinaigrette, mustard & honey 48–9

W

water 12

watercress, chorizo, & ricotta 98–9

wild garlic pesto 34

Y

yeast 12

Z

zucchini

  Gruyère & goat curd 84–6

  & ricotta 96–7

zucchini flowers 84–6

ACKNOWLEDGMENTS

Giuseppe and Bridget are both grateful to culinary figureheads from their pasts. In Giuseppe's case, the Neopolitan family kitchen was presided over by Geraldina Sepalone, his father's cook, who introduced him to the art of pizza and cooking in general. Bridget's baking inspiration was characterized by her grandmother, Lottie Dicks, who lived on a farm in a remote rural outpost in South Africa, where little could be bought and most things were made from scratch. In addition, both the authors would like to thank Marco Parente for his fundamental advice on dough, and Sita Devi for cleaning up after our mess while we were experimenting at home.

Disclaimer: *The information contained in this book is intended as a general guide. The curing recipes are based on the authors' own experimentation and research and neither the publisher nor the authors can be held responsible for the consequences of the application or misapplication of any of the information or ideas presented in this book.*

An Hachette UK Company
www.hachette.co.uk

First published in Great Britain in 2013 by Kyle Books, an imprint of Kyle Cathie Ltd
Carmelite House
50 Victoria Embankment
London EC4Y 0DZ
www.kylebooks.co.uk

This edition published in 2019.

ISBN: 978 0 85783 75 16

Distributed in the US by Hachette Book Group, 1290 Avenue of the Americas, 4th and 5th Floors, New York, NY 10104

Distributed in Canada by Canadian Manda Group, 664 Annette St., Toronto, Ontario, Canada M6S 2C8

Photography: Philip Webb
Design: Carl Hodson
Prop styling: Polly Webb Wilson
Food styling: Rosie Reynolds
Project editor: Judith Hannam
Editor: Vicki Murrell
Americanizer: Stephanie Schwartz
Production: Nic Jones, David Hearn and Lisa Pinnell

Library of Congress Control Number: 2015939766

Printed and bound in China

10 9 8 7 6 5 4 3 2 1